Advance Praise for *Hello (And Goodbye) To All That*

"Jonathan Liebson's book reflects an exceptional eye for seemingly ordinary yet uncanny events of day-to-day life, a prescient eye for drama that has a forgiving sense of humor, and a profound wisdom about people, contemporary culture, the cities and the world we live in, and basically everything that crosses a very gifted writer's mind."

—**André Aciman**,
Author of *Call Me by Your Name* and *Out of Egypt*

"In these humane, companionable stories, the trustworthy voice of author Jonathan Liebson captures the dilemma of a son trying to honor the heritage of his father, and a mensch trying to enact decency without resorting to self-righteousness."

—**Phillip Lopate**,
Author of *Bachelorhood* and Editor of *Writing New York* and *The Glorious American Essay*

"A unique, funny, and brutally honest perspective on living in New York City."

—**Jonah Hill**,
Oscar-Nominated Actor and Director

"The linked stories of family life and the coming awareness of a young man in Jonathan Liebson's *Hello (And Goodbye) To All That* are a poem of American life in the late 20th and early 21st century. Tender, beautiful, funny, and wise."

—**Rich Cohen**, Author of *New York Times* bestsellers *Tough Jews* and *The Sun & the Moon & the Rolling Stones*

"Minutely and wryly observed, like Vivian Gornick's *The Odd Woman and the City*, panoptic and kaleidoscopic, like Teju Cole's *Open City*, Jonathan Liebson's *Hello (And Goodbye) To All That* celebrates NYC in sentences built as beautifully as the city itself. Searching for the New York of his father's youth, Liebson finds instead a home of his own. His joy in living there—through all the chaos, street hassles, surprise tenderness, and cataclysms of the past three decades—will be his readers' joy too."

—**Heather Harpham**, Author of *Happiness: The Crooked Little Road to Semi-Ever After*

"Jonathan Liebson's *Hello (And Goodbye) To All That* is one of the great New York memoirs, updated for our day. In its ache, its beauty, and its energy, this book is a treasure to be read and re-read."

—**Mark Greif**, Author of
Against Everything: Essays

Hello (and goodbye) To All That

A MEMOIR OF A
CHANGING NEW YORK
IN THE
21ST CENTURY

Jonathan Liebson

A POST HILL PRESS BOOK
ISBN: 979-8-89565-037-0
ISBN (eBook): 979-8-89565-038-7

Hello (And Goodbye) To All That:
A Memoir of a Changing New York in the 21st Century

Cover design by Conroy Accord

This is a work of nonfiction. All people, locations, events, and situations are portrayed to the best of the author's memory.

Post Hill Press, LLC
New York • Nashville
posthillpress.com

Published in the United States of America
1 2 3 4 5 6 7 8 9 10

For my father, the true New Yorker

"...I pretended those were gaslights I saw in the streets below, that all old New Yorkers were my fathers, and that the train we waited for could finally take me back—back and back to that old New York of wood and brownstones and iron, where Theodore Roosevelt as Police Commissioner had walked every night."

–Alfred Kazin, *A Walker in the City*

Table of Contents

PART ONE

Second City to Second Avenue

Second Avenue Elevated

MY FATHER WAS A CARDIOLOGIST. In his top desk drawer he kept a stethoscope, a blood-pressure cuff, and stainless-steel calipers with needle-point tips. The calipers were a mapmaker's tool. Arms apart, they took measure of his patients' echocardiograms: opaque ultrasound images of a beating heart in space and time. Sometimes I would try on the floppy armband and pretend to guess my own blood pressure. A few quick squeezes brought the instrument to life. The armband fattened with air, the Velcro seal constricted my bicep, and the red needle danced and jiggled with equivocation. Thereafter I had no idea. I could squeeze, inflate, release—just like my father did—but I had no inkling how these actions fit together. It was like dealing out a hand of cards without the first clue how to play poker.

At 5:30 each morning he left home with a quick shave and a slap of cologne, but no shower. Sometimes I would hear his dress shoes on the front paving stones. Sometimes it was the muffled clap of the car door that awoke me. The starter winced—a begging that endured for several seconds until the engine turned over—and a fast shot of gas kept the car from falling back asleep. The tires reversed themselves over loose gravel, a strobe of headlights grazed my window shades, and I knew, as my father disappeared down the street, that his commute would take twice as long if he left any later. That much I grasped as a child, but I never understood how he could drag himself away so early without first dragging himself under hot water.

His preference was to take baths the night before. My father considered it a much more satisfying ritual at the end of his long day—and why not? Where else could a man go to be alone in his own house? Where else could he go to escape the ambient noise of the television, or to avoid talking with his wife?

"I'm taking a *baah-th*," he would announce on his way upstairs, affecting the voice of an Englishman. Ours was a split-level house. We had no master bathroom, only a second-level bathroom that was next to my brother's room and down the hall from my own. I heard three cranks of the faucet from inside, followed by the blast of water on porcelain. The water pooled in the tub with a low chugging sound, like that of the washing machine. My father stepped back into the hallway, and I instantly popped out to greet him. "Off with the dungarees," he said, tugging on his tie as he marched up the remaining seven steps. In his bedroom he would shrug off his good clothes and scan his bookshelves for something to read.

From the distant world of his hospital on Chicago's Near West Side, my father slipped seamlessly into his solitary life back home. His habit of reading was formed in childhood, where he'd fallen under the spell of such books as *The Wind in the Willows*, *There Was a Child Went Forth*, and the complete works of Sherlock Holmes. In college he squeezed his pre-med requirements between classes on history, philosophy, and the "Great Books" curriculum required of all students at Columbia University. On the toilet, in the leather chair of his bedroom study, or in the steamy, sequestered chamber of the bathtub, he read oversized books on the Celts, the Middle Ages, and World War II. He burrowed into Edmund Wilson's biographies of *The Thirties, The Forties, The Fifties*, and *The Sixties*; into the collected letters of E.B. White. One of his favorite books was *Joining the Club: A History of Jews and Yale*, which he read so many times that the soft cover permanently curled away from the other pages.

One time, over the sound of the bathroom vents, I knocked softly from the hallway and waited outside the door. No answer came, so I tried again. This time I knocked a little bit louder, and his mumbled reply I mistook for an invitation to enter.

"Yes?" he asked. His eyes slowly unfastened from the book he was reading. The splayed cover spread across his chest like a tanning reflector.

"Be careful—" I pointed. The book's bottom edge sat dangerously close to the waterline. Beneath the surface, his rounded belly split into a double image, his nakedness a few inches south.

"It's fine," he answered. His eyes drew back to the book—not out of concern, but from the pull of the next sentence. I stood there and waited, but he seemed to have already forgotten me. That was it: That was the beginning and end of our exchange. A sad and funny one to think about. A son intrudes on his father during bath time, but what kind of connection was he really hoping for? What conversation did he expect them to have? And the father, he behaves as if the son's sole reason for visiting is to warn him against soaking his book. Or, at least, he seems perfectly content to leave it at that. I mumbled goodbye as I closed the door behind me, and from the other side came the persistent humming of the bathroom vents.

History was more than a subject of books for my father. He was constantly invoking the past in his everyday life, as if to color in the lines of the present-day world. When my brother was an infant, his lower lip jutted out involuntarily, a mannerism my father likened to Winston Churchill. In imitation he would squint his eyes, turn out a shiny lip, and offer—in a gruffed-up voice—the prime minister's famous declaration: "We shall *neh*-vah, sur*ren*-dah, hrmph!" It was my father's version of Churchill's speech to the House of Commons in June of 1940, before the Battle of Britain. My father was only four years old at the time, so it had been much later when he heard a recording of the actual speech. My own likeness, he claimed, was to Woodrow Wilson. I had the president's thin face and square jaw, but because my father had never heard a recording of Wilson's voice, he never exclaimed to me how the right was more precious than the peace.

Though we walked through the same world, it was hard to see us as contemporaries. My father had one foot forever planted in the past. He'd grown up in what seemed like a golden age in New York City and a fabled time in our country's history. It was an era when the Yankees were synonymous with baseball, and baseball itself was still synonymous with America. How easy it was to romanticize that time period. Back then everyone had seemed more connected to one another, either by the neighborhoods they lived in or the programs they all listened to on the radio. In my own suburban childhood north of Chicago, that kind of connection seemed fleeting. People walled themselves off in large houses behind spacious front lawns; they drove cars on even the shortest of errands. It was true that technology made people more accessible in my day—fax machines and computers could hurtle us miles away in a matter of seconds—but I couldn't say whether that technology made the world feel smaller, or simply the people who used it. My father used that technology as well. He wore a pager on his hip, carried a portable phone in his car, and got to know computers through work. Yet these were merely instruments to him. I had the impression that my father only turned to them as needed. He never developed my own generation's dependence on the latest gadget, or our fixation on the next life-changing invention.

The few television programs that interested him were on Channel 11, Chicago's public TV station. The anthem for *Masterpiece Theatre* I easily recognized, its regal trumpets as unmistakable as the British accents or self-flattering dialogue. Occasionally, during dinner, my mother would announce a performance by Mark Russell later that night. He was a political comedian who stood on stage and told jokes to a live audience before he strolled over to his piano to play satirical songs. My parents laughed aloud at these. They had such a rollicking good time that I often joined in as well, even though the punch lines were beyond me. I was too young to understand what made Richard Nixon, Jimmy Carter, or Tip O'Neill so funny, but wasn't it comical enough to see a middle-aged man in a bow tie standing—rather than sitting—at a blue-painted piano decorated with white stars? His fingers zipped across the keyboard, his shoulders swooned, and his voice, just as he reached the chorus, would attain a wry, almost drunken pitch.

The other time we watched TV together was during the public television's weeklong fundraising drives. It seemed like every year the station would run some kind of documentary on the Second World War. In our family room my mother sat at one end of the fabric sofa, I at the other. My brother occupied the La-Z-Boy recliner while my father sat all by himself up front, at the edge of the blue shag area rug. He was barely four feet from the television. The rule was six feet—we kids had been told anything less was bad for our eyesight—but maybe that was a lie. Maybe it was because the TV was too irresistible up close, and our parents' best hope at restraining us was to keep us further away.

On the screen, Germany's Afrika Korps was being pushed back by the British Eighth Army. Rommel, the Desert Fox, had retreated from Egypt all the way to Algeria, some 1,750 miles, where he met the British First Army and a division of Americans. In a later image, General Eisenhower was shown riding in a jeep with General Omar Bradley, the two men inspecting US positions in Tunisia. My father was so close that the light of the TV reflected off his face. He sat cross-legged, rocking back and forth as he chewed his tongue. His hands scratched each other anxiously. His knuckles were like walnuts, his skin chafed from the bite of his fingernails. "Stop it," my brother and I both said. His agitation filled the room, as if he were receiving reports directly from the front lines. "*Phil—*" our mother shouted, and he finally glanced up in self-awareness. He pulled his hands apart and stifled them at his sides, only to resume scratching a few moments later.

Most of what we watched on television my father had actually lived through. He was born in 1936 and grew up at the end of the Depression. To someone who'd never experienced it, the very word "Depression" had a romantic flavor. It evoked images of apple sellers in the streets, of people shining shoes, taking odd jobs, and doing whatever they could to survive. I envisioned a frontier spirit in my father's day, an attitude reminiscent of America's earliest settlers. The pictures I saw all seemed to communicate the same message: Out of great hardship, its opposite was born. I believed such low points were crucial to our country's success, like a collective ladder we used to elevate ourselves. This was a safe, easy notion for a suburban child to have, particularly one who'd never been part of the climb.

My father had been. He was too young to fight in the Second World War, but he'd been alive to witness the last of the great emancipators. He described a newsreel he'd seen of FDR and Churchill talking, when he was five years old. He thought their voices sounded out of the ordinary—"not like people you met on the street," he said. "It was as if they had bread in her mouths." Later, while he was a medical resident, my father served as an officer in the Navy. He was drafted in August of 1961, after the Soviet Union closed off East Berlin, though he didn't receive his commission until July of 1962, almost one year later. Only a few months afterward he heard rumors that America was going to war. His destroyer, the *USS Buck*, had been docked in Seattle that October, during the World's Fair. Kennedy was scheduled to visit them on a Sunday, but at the last moment he mysteriously called off sick. Everyone became suspicious. On Monday, news broke out about the Cuban Missile Crisis. Just before his destroyer shoved off, my father called home to tell his mom goodbye. He said he didn't know when they would talk again.

To me it sounded heroic. My father had been cast in one of the great installments of the Cold War. Experience told otherwise. In the end, their destroyer had only been sent to Treasure Island, in San Francisco Bay, on orders to protect the Golden Gate Bridge from enemy ships. For two weeks my father took day trips into San Francisco, while the bridge remained safely guarded from Fidel Castro and the Soviets.

These stories, which I grew up hearing and rehearing, left me feeling cheated by my own birth. I was a late arrival to the twentieth century. I'd been relegated to a prosperous and unpolemical age, whereas my father was the product of a glorified past. It was a past he remained devoted to. His two greatest passions were baseball and the New York City transit lines of his childhood. Surprisingly, he was not a Yankees fan. As a boy he'd been to Yankee Stadium, but his interest in baseball grew out of the first World Series he ever heard on the radio. This was in October of 1945, a couple years after his family had left Manhattan and moved to Forest Hills, Queens. In that Series the Detroit Tigers were taking on the Chicago Cubs (our very own Cubs!). At PS 3 (Public School Three), his phys ed teacher, Mr. Dufferin, had the game turned on. "All the boys listened to the Series," my father said. "All the girls were sewing." That Series went the distance—a full seven games—with the Tigers eventually defeating the Cubs and my father becoming a lifelong fan. He chose wisely. The Cubs wouldn't make it back to the World Series until 2016, over seventy-five years later.

Most nights after dinner he would check out from the rest of us. Rooted to his desk chair, he hunched forward like some medieval scribe as he pored over an enormous baseball encyclopedia. The massive book sat humped in front of him: a cascade of figures and numbers hoarded into various alignment on the tissue-thin pages. On a large legal pad he copied down pages upon pages of these statistics. He never saved the sheets themselves but remarkably held on to the information. He knew home-run titles, batting averages, pennant winners, win-loss records of pitchers that went back many decades. He enjoyed being tested on all the great players: the Tigers' Hank Greenberg, "Doc" Cramer, and Hal Newhouser; the Yankees'

Joe DiMaggio, Yogi Berra, and Phil Rizzuto; and from the old Brooklyn Dodgers, Gil Hodges, Duke Snider, and Jackie Robinson. He was a giant receptacle of facts, which included hometowns, birthdates, and funny stories. My high school homeroom teacher was from Anderson, Indiana, which my father never failed to remind him was the same hometown of Carl Erskine, a right-handed pitcher for the Brooklyn and then Los Angeles Dodgers.

Casey Stengel, the Yankees manager from 1949 to 1960, was another common reference. Like Yogi Berra, he was famous for his quizzical and often humorous statements. My dad mentioned an interview once in which Stengel was asked whether staying away from alcohol helped baseball players. His answer: only if they could already play. In another story, the manager was said to approach his left-fielder in the dugout one day, where he casually mentioned some "news" that might be of interest to him. Turning to his player, Stengel supposedly said, "Well, one of us has just been traded to Kansas City."

The stories my father told were more interesting than the straight facts, but he always seemed to care more about the trivia. He begged to be quizzed on dates and figures. Sometimes he would recite these in public or in front of my friends. "What else?" he'd say. "Ask me more." He became ravenous. Once the data started pouring out, he lost all self-control. My mother rebuked him for showing off. My brother and I both became embarrassed. And still, no matter how annoying he got—or how often we intervened to pull the plug—we retained a secret pride in him. It was hard, in spite of this overbearing behavior, not to be awed by his immense knowledge.

Below the baseball encyclopedias, the bottom shelves of his twin bookcases were lined with such titles as *New York in the Thirties* and *Lost New York*; photography books like *Changing New York* by Berenice Abbott and *Of New York* by André Kertész. The tall hardcovers had inch-thick bindings; a single book could stand freely if I nudged the cover open the slightest bit. These books showed pictures and told stories of the subways and elevated trains that had been around in my father's lifetime. The one he most often referred to was a thin, modest-looking soft-cover called *Second Avenue El in Manhattan*. The cover showed the Fiftieth Street Station facing north. "Pickwick Pharmacy was one block away," he told me. That was my grandfather's old drugstore, on 51st Street and Second Avenue. My grandfather had bought the pharmacy in 1920, inheriting the name "Pickwick" from the Pickwick Arms Hotel just down the street. On the wall of my dad's study hung a picture of my grandfather behind the drugstore counter. He wore a white frock as he held a phone in one hand and worked a mortar and pestle in the other, filling someone's order. Several rows of apothecary jars lined the shelves of the back wall, some of which had migrated to the entryway of our house. The original of that photograph, I learned, had appeared on the cover of *American Druggist* magazine in 1951.

Of the Pickwick Arms Hotel, my father said with great import that the writer John O'Hara had lived there. I didn't tell him that I'd never heard of O'Hara, let alone read any of his work. But I *had* heard of another famous writer from the neighborhood. John Steinbeck lived on 51st Street in the early 1940s, though my father himself hadn't known this at the time. He never suspected, when he saw the film *Tortilla Flat* advertised at the local movie house, that the author himself lived just down the street.

Numerous celebrities frequented Pickwick Pharmacy. One morning, someone entered the drugstore wearing a sharp suit and fedora, and the entire place went suddenly quiet. People stopped what they were doing to gawk at this important-looking individual, while my father, only five years old, asked my grandfather who the man was. My grandfather looked around with some embarrassment. He leaned down to my father and said: "That's no man—that's Greta Garbo!" Years later, my father would occasionally see the actor Anthony Perkins, whose family my dad was acquainted with. One day he innocently asked Perkins how his mother was doing, only to see the man laugh inexplicably. My father had made an inside joke—except he wasn't in on it. He didn't realize that the movie *Psycho* had just come out, and he had no idea about the old lady Norman Bates kept in the attic.

His first apartment in the city was at 311 51st Street, less than a half block from Pickwick Pharmacy. "Three hundred and six feet," my father stated. He cited the figure as though he'd measured it on hands and knees. The number stuck in his head like all the other dates and facts he recited: as incontrovertible as the batting averages or win-loss records in any of his encyclopedias. In 1941, his family moved a few blocks away to East 48th Street between First Avenue and the East River, where they remained another two years before moving to Forest Hills. That second apartment no longer exists, as it was torn down to make way for the UN.

Near these first two apartments was the Second Avenue Elevated, a train for which my father developed a special affinity. On the soft-cover jacket of that particular book, a one-story rectangular cabin stands at the edge of the elevated platform. It was the switching tower that used to send the trains back to Queens. Just beyond the tracks, a blank white billboard framed the top corner of an apartment building. My father recalled how he and his friends would watch from the street as men on raised platforms periodically repainted the sign. "Every couple of months they would change the ad," he said. "But it was always for Sunkist oranges." *Could this really be true*, I wondered? The same product each and every time? I had no proof against my father's memory.

As a young boy, my father and his family would take the Second Avenue line to Coney Island. He was very particular in recounting his journey. The El cost five cents back then. At Park Row, in lower Manhattan, they changed to the elevated Culver Line of the BMT (short for Brooklyn-Manhattan Transit), which crossed over the Brooklyn Bridge. He was too small for the rides at the amusement park (except the merry-go-round), so he and his parents spent most of their time at the beach. They also took the Second Avenue El to see the 1939 World's Fair, in Flushing Meadows–Corona Park. For this they rode in the other direction, crossing over the 59th Street Bridge into Queens. Every few months, my father told me, he and his parents would take the El down to the same delicatessen on the Lower East Side. That was his father's old neighborhood. Edward had been born near Odessa, in the Ukraine, in 1892, and came to America in 1900. My grandfather had lived on Norfolk and Rivington Street, an area that in the early twentieth century was teeming with Jews and populated with synagogues. (Many of those old synagogues remain, though they're now defunct.) According to my father, the deli wasn't anything grand. He described a corner entrance with tables along each street-side window, an unswept terrazzo floor, and large salamis strung up above the deli counter. He never ordered corned beef, pastrami, or any of the other delights you might expect. He always ate "the special"—which was nothing more than a large hot dog. I asked him: Why such a fancy name for something so simple? My father had no answer. He ordered two specials with a side of fries and Dr. Brown's Cel-Ray Soda, a celery-flavored soft drink that came in a can.

My father enjoyed the food but not the delicatessen. The restaurant—in fact, the entire neighborhood—made him uncomfortable. At the deli, the female waitress would hurry around, shouting the customers' orders at the top of her lungs. "I didn't understand why she had to yell so loud," he said. "She wouldn't stop." (Forty years later, that same deli would pass into popular culture, as another woman's screams were depicted there in the movie *When Harry Met Sally.*) Afterward, as he and his parents walked the Lower East Side, my dad was put off by the bustling, inhospitable streets. "Sunday was the busiest day," he said. People with raised voices rushed in all directions, the streets were even more crowded than the deli. He and his parents wandered past stores selling tobacco, housewares, and clothing. Everything about the neighborhood seemed foreign to him. Vendors sold pickles from wooden barrels, store windows were painted with indecipherable letters, and the Jews—with their black clothing, hanging tzitzit, and ringleted hair—looked nothing like the Jews he knew.

"We were different from them," he told me. "My father had come from there, but he was a quiet man. He dressed neatly and he never rushed." The "there" he meant was the Lower East Side, but I suspected, somehow, that he was really talking about someplace else—the Eastern Europe from which his ancestors hailed—and I attributed his distaste to the *shtetels* in which these Jews once lived. That certainly explained my own revulsion. These ghettos were a blemish on our past, and it baffled me why Jews would cross an ocean and resettle in the New World, only to import that same old culture with them. What point in speaking the same tongue and wearing the same strange clothing that divided you from your fellow countrymen? To see pictures of those neighborhoods was to be reminded of the atrocities that befell so many of their relatives back in Europe. And it felt, in some dark corner of my mind, like an invitation to the same treatment over here.

The documentaries on television gave profound glimpses into that mistreatment. I shuddered at the images of rail-thin people, barely human-looking, who wore striped vestments adorned with the Star of David. How frightening to think this frail condition—with their bodies reduced to scarecrows—was actually the lesser of evils awaiting them. During my father's childhood, people were certainly aware of Hitler. Everyone talked about the war in Europe, he told me, but the real horrors in Germany and Poland were still largely unknown. In reality—and in the worst of anyone's imagination—such horrors remained unfathomable.

For my father, one of the great casualties of the war, albeit unrelated, was the closing of the Second Avenue Elevated. The portion that ran above 59th Street shut down on June 11, 1940. "That was the day the Germans entered Paris," said my father. He'd been four years old at the time. "It was the same day that Italy declared war on France," he added, and here he copped Churchill's voice again. My father spoke in a low, bit-off snarl, calling Mussolini a "whipped jackal" who came "frisking at the side of the German Tiger with yelpings of triumph." The imitation, I thought, sounded vaguely like W.C. Fields. On June 13, 1942, the rest of the Second Avenue El shut down. That was one week after the Battle of Midway, my father informed me.

Many years later, I would finally hear a recording of Churchill's voice. The audio quality was poor, and through the rumpled static he sounded less commanding than what I had expected. It was certainly not the voice you'd associate with such a hulking figure. And yet it was impossible, as Churchill drew toward the end of his speech, not to be moved by his words. I felt a stir of anticipation when he declared: "We shall fight in the fields, and in the streets, we shall fight in the hills…." My ears perked up, and I waited for his exclamatory *hrmph!*—… only it never came. Had I missed it? I replayed that portion again, straining to hear through the background muck, but it wasn't there. At last I had to face reality: Either that exclamation had been invented by my father, or he must've grafted it from another of Churchill's speeches.

I never mentioned this to him. It would've been wrong to call out the mistake—like contesting a history that wasn't mine to begin with. That version of my father's story remained as true to him as any of the dates or events etched in his mind; as real as any of the old photographs from his books. To my father, those photographs bore an animation beyond the page, while Churchill had been an actual living figure in his own lifetime. To me, these images were something out of folklore, while Churchill was a symbol from a bygone era. The same could be said of Eisenhower and Kennedy—names I associated with Chicago expressways as much as former presidents. To this day, the word "Midway" still evokes a distant, hard-to-reach airport on Chicago's South Side, versus the famous battle it was meant to honor.

My father's past cast a long shadow from a place forever beyond the horizon. Pickwick Pharmacy, the Second Avenue Elevated, my grandfather Edward—they were all ghosts to me. "You have his hands," my father often insisted. "I'm telling you—you *do*." But he was only half-speaking to me. I sensed his attention lay elsewhere: in a backward glance I could never share with him. I both envied and resented my father for his connection to history, in the same way a pauper both envies and resents the rich: for all their unobtainable possessions. It didn't matter how many stories he shared about my grandfather, he couldn't resurrect a man I'd never known. And it didn't matter how many tales he told about New York City, I couldn't imagine my grandfather's pharmacy on a corner now occupied by an Italian restaurant, or a throng of Jews in place of all those tourists at Katz's Deli, or the Brooklyn Dodgers playing anywhere but in Los Angeles.

There and Back Again

My first memory of New York is a giant room with painted blue walls and a ceiling that's impossibly high. I can't make out the faces around me, but I sense the blur of children scampering about, the commotion of unchecked voices. A handful of adults, restless and observant, hover somewhere in the background. It's a scene that would visit me multiple times in childhood: a recurring dream that made me suspect at some point that this place might really exist. "Oh, sure," my parents told me, "that's the playroom at Payson House." Payson House was the high-rise apartment on East 70th Street near York Avenue, where I'd lived between the ages of one and two-and-a-half. It wasn't the only image I recalled from that time period. The other was of a swimming pool set high in the air, surrounded by a vast blue sky. The setting was so foreign to my suburban Chicago home that I assumed I must've invented it. But this, too, shared a foothold in reality. My mother told me of an apartment swimming pool some thirty-five floors above street level—although she insisted that the pool was above ground, not the sunken kind. For some reason that detail never registered with my young brain, so it failed to make the trip with me to Illinois.

I was born in New York University Hospital, on East 30th and First Avenue, and spent my first two-and-a-half years on the Upper East Side, before my father moved us to the Midwest. He was a lifelong New Yorker: Manhattan for his first seven years, then Queens, then Manhattan again (minus a two-year stint in the Navy). He remained in his home city for college, medical school, his residency in internal medicine, his fellowship in cardiology, and then as an assistant professor at New York Hospital and Cornell University. He finally left for a job at Rush-Presbyterian-St. Luke's Hospital in Chicago, a move in which he traded the hurly-burly of Manhattan for the more tranquil suburbs; the unswimmable East River for the unbearable cold of Lake Michigan; and the subways he knew backward and forward for the sprawling and ever-congested commuter highways.

New York would come into gradual focus for me. I took a few early trips there with my family, during which several scenes imprinted themselves on my memory. In one visit we went to see my father's mother, Grandma Sarah, who lived in the same apartment in Forest Hills, Queens, where my father had grown up. I was taken aback by the size of her. Sarah was an enormous woman with pink, pasty skin, a raspy voice, and a domineering personality that my mother made strategic reference to in her arguments with my dad. As vivid to me as my grandmother's face was her scratchy voice and the aged, lived-in odor of her apartment. It was a smell that combined something of her own physical scent with the cloistered bric-a-brac of her living room. Needless to say, I couldn't get out of there fast enough.

The real New York was Manhattan, of course. I recall visiting my father's former colleague from Cornell, a chemistry researcher whose wife my mom had befriended and whose daughter was close to me in age. The father was far from how you'd picture a scientist. He stood at least six feet tall, smoked cigarettes, had a lanky swagger like the Marlboro Man, greeted you with an iron handshake, and drank Scotch from a tumbler that disappeared in his giant hand. He was the kind of man who charmed and intimidated you at the same time. I remember thinking his apartment was small in comparison to his overgrown stature, and a little too modest for his outsized personality. As a child of suburban Chicago, I had no way to gauge the size of Manhattan dwellings, and it would be many years before I realized my mistake.

The crowded sidewalks of Midtown were both dizzying and enthralling. The city had an endless supply of yellow cabs, a fleet that was newly replenished with each green light. In storefront windows, the taxi's checkerboard strip was nearly as ubiquitous, appearing in miniature over a yellow-and-black background of coffee ads for Chock full o'Nuts. My favorite treat was the New York pretzel. Its alluring, ever-present smell is lost to today's city goers. So, too, is the musty, doughy, leathery-knuckled pretzel of yore. Drawn by metal tongs from the steaming bowels of a pretzel cart, pressed face-down into a vat of salt, the pretzel came delivered in a white tissue that warmed your hand. Here was the original street food. A pretzel was meant to be consumed outdoors, one chewy piece at a time, whether you strolled through the park, sat on a bench, or stood right there on the sidewalk.

One night, when we were walking back to our hotel, we noticed a group of onlookers in a small plaza below Central Park. Floodlights trained on a beautiful young woman wearing a glamorous dress and glittering wrap. The fountain she posed beside was cordoned off from bystanders, and the woman seemed remarkably unbothered by all the attention. She smiled, posted a hand on her hip, took a short walk beside the cistern, gave a flick of her hair. It turned out she was being filmed for a TV commercial. I marveled at the whole setup of lights and cameras—and at witnessing in person what would one day end up on television. And yet, even then the thrill was balanced by a sense of how ordinary it seemed. Many spectators were already starting to peel off, and I suspected that this was simply one more incident a person might stumble on, or stumble past, as they made their way through the city.

For college I looked to the Northeast, where both my parents had done their studies. The Columbia of my father's era was a storied place. Its president at the time, Dwight D. Eisenhower, went on to occupy the White House, while luminaries like Allen Ginsburg and Jack Kerouac went on to occupy the public's imagination. The place I visited seemed far removed from that vibrant past. In the late 1980s, Columbia's prim campus was in need of much refurbishment. Two tennis courts with chain-link fencing made for an eyesore in the main quad, as did a rash of scaffolding that blanketed one of the high-rises. Rightly or wrongly, Columbia felt like a commuter college squeezed into the city. It lacked the bucolic spaciousness and sense of being physically set apart that I saw in other campuses. The openness of those physical settings—from the sprawling green lawns to the surrounding hillsides—somehow seemed essential to the mind's own ability to stretch out and expand. Alas, my poor father: Neither of his sons would attend his alma mater.

The liberal arts college I went to in Connecticut was flooded with students from the New York area, and against this large contingency I maintained a fierce allegiance to the Windy City.

I boasted about its sports heroes (Walter Payton and Michael Jordan), its deep-dish pizza, its beautiful lakefront skyline (which owned the world's tallest building), and its hometown movies like *Risky Business* and *Ferris Bueller's Day Off*. A few years later, after a semester in Paris and a couple trips to my friend's home in Greenwich Village, I would start to change my tune. Chicago's skyline was still number one in my book, and I still appreciated its world-class museums, but in these other cities I felt a sense of freedom that was lacking in Chicago. The El was great for commuting downtown or going to Cubs games, but unless you were heading due north or south, it wasn't likely to take you where you needed. By contrast, from Greenwich Village I could walk a few blocks, pop down into the subway, and pop back up within a stone's throw of Central Park or the Met, or in the heart of Chinatown. Those underground trains felt like the lifeblood of the city, connecting its far-flung neighborhoods and making them accessible to both visitors and inhabitants alike.

The pull of New York grew stronger toward the end of college, but I once again turned away from it. As students strode around campus from interview to interview, abandoning their jeans and baseball caps for suits and ties, I pretended an interest in the whole job process. Having built a résumé of internships, I fell under the delusion that recruiters should try to win *me* over, and not vice versa. In one interview for an investment bank, after the woman asked how I would describe the position I was applying for, I smiled and said I'd been hoping *she* would describe the position to me. The woman smiled back politely in a way that told me the interview was over.

We were well rid of each other. Was there anything further from my mind at that point than finding a real job? After having my world opened up in the classroom and a semester overseas, why would I suddenly throw myself onto the treadmill? A college friend had shared the startling advice of his creative writing professor, who'd offered her students an unconventional reason to memorize poetry. She'd told them that if they were ever in a car crash and laying by the side of the road, they could always recite poetry in their head while waiting for the ambulance to come. Wouldn't that ambulance come for us all one day? Before mine did, I wanted to make sure I had a lot more poetry in me.

So I went back to Paris. I saved money at home that summer and then took another unpaid internship that fall, this one in the tiny bureau of ABC News. It was a desk-jockey position with no chance of advancement, but the experience did provide an important highlight. That November we covered the American presidential election at a gathering of ex-pats at the Hotel Concorde, and with no responsibilities to speak of, I spent several hours eating, drinking, and mingling with a college friend while we watched the results come in. As the sun came up over Paris, we escaped to the balcony and gazed out over the quiet, empty streets. A dreaminess took hold of us, and after another toast to Bill Clinton's victory, my friend informed me of his big decision: He was leaving Paris for his native Ohio to start work on a screenplay.

It would take me another few months to leave. I inherited my friend's waitering job at a fifties-style American diner, a place with red leather booths, neon signs for Route 66, and photographs of James Dean and vintage Pan Am airliners. Working the extended lunch shift, I made a good wage that put real money in my pocket, but I also felt an increasing restlessness that wouldn't go away. In our middle-of-the-night phone calls, my Ohio friend would update me on the progress of his screenplay, which I never doubted would get made into a movie. The more he spoke about it, the more I began to wonder: What was my own next step supposed to be?

My parents, it turned out, were just as anxious about my future. When I finally came home that spring, I had barely unpacked my bags before they cornered me. What exactly was I planning to do now? I'd gotten good grades in school, had interned for a highly respected senator (Paul Simon, who shared his famous name with the singer of "The Boxer"), yet nothing as clear-cut as a job or law school seemed to be looming. I didn't have a good answer for them. When they continued to pester me, I finally got testy in return. If they were so worried about my life, how did they think *I* felt? It was *my* life, after all.

I brought my frustrations to the parents of a close friend, who listened patiently in their den as I offered up a mouthful of excuses and hesitations. When his turn finally came, my friend's dad looked at me and said, "You know, Jon, if there were a better word for it, they wouldn't call it *work*." He said this without sarcasm or any trace of condescension, and it remains among the wisest, most compassionate advice I've ever heard.

And yet it couldn't derail me from my wayward track. Over the years I would continue to move about, crisscrossing the country, heading back overseas, staying at my parents' house in between destinations. I caddied, delivered pizza, did office work, and became a grunt on my friend's low-budget film in Ohio. For six months I lived in Socorro, New Mexico, working as a night clerk at the Econolodge while writing a terrible knock-off of Steinbeck's *Cannery Row*. I did a master's of literature in England, then moved down to Charleston, South Carolina, hoping to experience the South I'd read about in William Faulkner. It was a South that didn't exist in progressive

Charleston. A year and a half later I headed to Miami of Ohio for their master's program in creative writing. If not Oxford, Mississippi, then at least I'd get Oxford, Ohio—which was close in spirit to another writer I admired: Sherwood Anderson.

Along the way, I made occasional layovers in New York City. I stayed in my friend's high-rise apartment (his parent's apartment, that is) on Bleecker Street, in that trio of ugly concrete towers designed by I.M. Pei. We ate two-dollar falafel at Mamoun's on MacDougal Street; we went to John's Pizza on Bleecker near Seventh Avenue, with its wide ovens perched in back and celebrity photographs adorning the walls. We killed time at Tower Records on Broadway and East 4th Street; for late night antics we hung out at the Olive Tree Cafe on MacDougal, a dark restaurant with a somewhat bohemian feel, where you scribbled with chalk on the tables and watched Charlie Chaplain films projected onto the walls. To use the bathroom you had to pass downstairs through the comedy cellar, always in fear of drawing attention from whatever comic was on stage.

Before I'd left Charleston for Miami of Ohio, an incredible thing happened. I'd been working that spring as an adjunct professor at the College of Charleston and a night clerk at Atlantic Books on East Bay Street. The used bookstore stood along a lovely promenade near the harbor, close to the historic mansions of the Battery and a number of high-end restaurants, and in that way the store drew just enough nighttime tourists to keep the doors open. One evening, I got to talking with a soft-spoken gentleman with a kind, scholarly air. The man was a dean at The University of the South—also known as Sewanee—a grand old institution that a friend in Charleston had graduated from. The man and I conversed about his storied university, its prestigious literary journal, Southern authors we liked, and the writing program I would attend in the fall. That alone had made for a good night, as the job's real payoff lay in the interesting customers who sometimes wandered inside. Another one was waiting in the wings. No sooner had the man walked out than another gentleman came over to introduce himself.

His accent was also Southern, albeit different from the other man's. He owned a deep, graveled voice with a stronger twang and a commanding tone that was seasoned by military experience. He'd overheard me talking about MFA programs and wondered if I'd considered applying to New York University. Of course I had. Not only was the program highly regarded, but one of my favorite authors—E.L. Doctorow—taught there. NYU had a serious drawback, however: It offered little money to graduate students. The man nodded, and without missing a beat he said, "Yes, but you can get funding through my department." He spoke as if he were ready to hand over the money right then. Had he been a genie, he might've added: "And what about your other two wishes?"

It turned out that this man who'd been vacationing on Kiawah Island, and who'd dropped in to Charleston for dinner, was also the head of the Expository Writing Program at NYU. The department drew its teachers from across the spectrum of graduate students, offering them a tuition waiver and a small stipend. I was beside myself with excitement. Of course, the deadline for next year's applications had long since passed, but I promised to keep that information in mind. Even then, the question had already presented itself: Could MFA students transfer to another program? It was a longshot path that I never really expected to come true, just as I never doubted that at some point I would have to give it a try.

Miami of Ohio is a stunning red-brick campus set among rolling hills and expansive cornfields. When I first laid eyes on it, I thought the college contained as much red brick as Harvard Yard. The undergrads were a mixture of overachieving students from Ohio and other Midwestern states, plus some more parochial students from rural parts of Ohio. I'd like to think I gave the writing program a chance. I had some wonderful and committed teachers there, and I also made two great friends. One was a gifted short story writer from Texas, a second-year student who to this day remains a North Star for me. The other was an evangelical Christian, a woman whose deep faith was of the kind I'd only ever witnessed once before: in my mother's mother (*Bubbie*, we called her in Yiddish). This student had a large personality, spoke eloquently, and would pray for people whose views differed from her own—even those whose behavior she found objectionable (a category I sometimes fell into). I'd never met anyone so tolerant, nor had I ever imagined an evangelical who possessed the nimble intellect of a college debater—something she'd actually been. We engaged in deep discussions, believer to nonbeliever, and never once did she shut down an argument by making a quick retreat into scripture, something that a number of my students had done in their essays.

The huge influence of these two individuals could not make up for the general dissatisfaction I felt. My Texas friend would be graduating that year, as would the next-closest writer of talent, and thereafter came a sizeable drop-off in ability (myself included). Just as crucially, I felt a serious drop-off in commitment. I longed for the company of writers who believed in the dire importance of what they were doing—who understood that we were in training, not just passing time. My deficiencies were plentiful, and I thought that a workshop of more talented writers was no less essential than hitting around with better tennis players: something that would help raise the level of my own game.

So I sent out a handful of transfer applications that winter, including to the program in Iowa City, which offered a place to my Texas friend but turned me down (the right choice on their part). NYU's application was the only one in which I included a work of creative nonfiction: a piece about my Chicago childhood set against the backdrop of my father's stories of growing up in New York City. It was called "Second Avenue Elevated," a piece I would not return to for many years. By the time the program got around to accepting me, I'd already won a fellowship to teach Expository Writing. (The director had stepped aside and let two other faculty interview me.) My Texas friend couldn't have been happier, but my evangelical friend didn't hide her disappointment. And yet, amazingly, she told me that she had nevertheless prayed for me to get in. I don't know if I was more astonished or touched by this confession. To this day I still credit her—and her prayers—for the good fortune that came my way.

In the summer that followed, I divided my time between Oxford, Ohio, and Wilmette, Illinois. I made the five-hour trip multiple times, using my mother's old Ford Escort, and in mid-July I flew out East for a week and stayed with a friend's older brother near St. Mark's Place and Second Avenue. At that point, I embarked on a project that made getting into an MFA program seem like a cakewalk: I began looking for a decent place to live in New York City.

A View of the Village

By the time I moved to New York, I had reached a point in my life where I considered the days of roommates and loft beds far behind me. The city quickly brought these back into play. I arrived for a week in mid-July of 1998, purchased the weekly unlimited MetroCard for seventeen dollars, and hoped to secure a place for August, before my MFA program began. I scoured the listings in the *Village Voice* (the print edition dropped on Wednesday, though many listings came online Tuesday night), made endless phone calls, and tried to keep track of everything in a notepad. I saw bedrooms that were divided in half by a curtain; bedrooms you obtained by first passing through someone else's; railroad apartments (so-called because of their rail thinness) with a central corridor closely straddled by closet-size rooms. In one apartment share, the guy admitted I'd be covering the full rent—mine plus his—as he used his own share to pay his grandmother's expenses. I admired his honesty almost as much as I resented him for it. Even the plum one-bedroom I was crashing in, which belonged to the older brother of a childhood friend, had a strange setup. The East Village apartment was entirely his for the majority of the year, except during the occasional, unannounced visits by the lease holder, who flew in from Puerto Rico and stayed an indeterminate number of days.

I learned what the term "walk-up" meant. Stupidly, I had somehow believed it stood for a building with a short staircase in front—otherwise known as a stoop. (This would not be my dumbest mistake about New York architecture, which was soon to come.) In reality, a walk-up meant nothing more than a building without an elevator. That definition rang true to me as I climbed narrow staircases with rickety, sagging stairs that arrived at shoebox apartments barely a step above squalor. I saw units with a shower in the kitchen, kitchens that were sink-less and had but a hotplate and a mini-fridge, apartments whose bathroom belonged to a shared common hallway. In Paris I had seen such conditions—the worst being those former maid's quarters on the top floor, with their old-style shitters (*chiottes*) that had grooved foot pads where you squatted over a hole in the floor. But never had I anticipated such widespread decrepitude in modern New York. It might not have been the tenement era of Jacob Riis, but it didn't feel like much progress.

I had been hoping to pay my own way, even on a tiny stipend, but I soon despaired at the unlikelihood. My father immediately offered to help out. "I don't want you living in a flytrap," he said, and I was touched by the firmness of his concern, even as the term "flytrap" made me bristle with shame.

More than once, I recalled something that an older college friend had told me. When I shared with him my potential literary interests, this econ major and future investment banker responded with a riddle: "What do you call a publisher in New York City?" he asked. I shrugged and said I didn't know, so he leaned closer and whispered: "Poor." He spat the word out like a bad taste in his mouth. His prophecy put me in mind of an old

New Yorker cartoon, which shows a young man in jeans, blazer, and bare feet who sits slumped on a sofa across from his father: an elegant man in a suit and cravat who's seated comfortably in a stuffed armchair. Stroking a cat in his lap, the father projects an air of mild, aristocratic indifference as he remarks to his son: "Of course, the examined life doesn't pay very much, does it?"

I learned quickly that in New York City, everyone spent more than what their bank account said they should. Everyone compromised one set of priorities for another, and everyone seemed willing to sacrifice so much for a city that seemed so willing to reject them. And yet, after a dismal week of apartment hunting, a ray of sunshine came my way. I visited an affordable and legitimate two-bedroom at the Stuyvesant Town complex on the East Side, a unit belonging to a thirty-three-year-old public attorney who said she preferred a male roommate. She was intelligent, quick-witted, and—I chose not to mind—flirtatious. After we'd hit it off, I left with the impression that the place was essentially mine. Finally, I had caught the break I was looking for! Not so fast. By next morning, I learned that someone else was ahead of me in line: a friend of a friend who'd come out of a bad breakup. I remained the lawyer's preferred choice, but if the other person wanted it then the apartment would be hers. For several more days she kept me hovering between hope and dejection, until—in spite of my well-made arguments and impassioned pleas—I lost my case.

When I returned in mid-August for my teacher training, I crashed on a friend's sofa on Cornelia Street between Bleecker and West 4th. I was forced to endure another two weeks of frustration before I finally settled for a temporary sublet on Sullivan Street, for $600 a month. It was a share, of course: two side-by-side bedrooms that opened onto a small kitchen area with a breakfast bar but no table. The common space was further reduced by a bulging TV atop the counter, where my roommate, a woman in her mid-twenties, watched episodes of *The Nanny* over dinner. If it wasn't the voice of Fran Drescher invading my bedroom, it was the curry smells of Green Papaya, a Thai restaurant on the building's ground floor, or else the after-hours noise of drunken revelers and honking horns. Just around the corner, the Life Club expelled its partygoers as late as 2 a.m. on weeknights, while a stop sign at Bleecker Street gave cross traffic the infinite right of way. Sometimes, the waiting cars on Sullivan backed up all the way to the end of the block, and the immobilized drivers would share their profanity with the entire neighborhood.

The noise, the cramped kitchen, the close-to-intolerable roommate—what did I have to complain about? I was living in Greenwich Village, just a few blocks from Washington Square Park and a short five-minute walk to my classes. I was near The Front Page, MacDougal Café, Mamoun's—all the places I'd frequented in my visits to the city. Also nearby was the venerable Caffé Reggio, a place where my father used to meet his own friends or just read by himself, when he lived in Forest Hills. My friend hosting me on Cornelia Street had told me not to obsess about living in the Village, saying that New Yorkers quickly grew accustomed to taking the subway. It was smart, well-intended advice, but I'd strongly resisted it. To someone on a limited budget, your home turf seemed all the more important. The ability to open your door in the vicinity of your favorite hangouts, and to delight in your neighborhood merely by walking around it, allowed you to meet the city just a little bit more on your own terms. Which was what I did.

In the fall of 1998, pay phones marked all the street corners in New York City. Cell phones existed in the hands of a relative few, while the device of choice for business professionals and journalists was the BlackBerry. Its unique feature—a small screen with a mini alphabetic keypad—was to receive and send emails on the go. The drop of a token got you through the subway turnstile, though the MetroCard existed for unlimited daily, weekly, or monthly rides ($4, $17, and $31, respectively). The average cost of a pizza slice was a dollar fifty, while the best slice in the city, at least to many people in the environs of Greenwich Village, cost $1.85. That honor went to Joe's Pizza, a little stand on Father Demo Square, just a few steps from Bleecker Street. At Katz's Deli, on East Houston and First Avenue, a pastrami sandwich cost a whopping $8.25, though it was worth every penny. Some maintained that Second Avenue Deli had the superior sandwich, a claim that the owners clearly put stock in, as the restaurant saw fit to charge $10.75 for their own version.

At the foot of Manhattan, the city's Twin Towers stood like giant masts at the island's stern. These two rectangular pegs were neither attractive nor inspiring structures. They lacked the majesty of Chicago's Sears Tower (the world's tallest building at the time) or the elegant finishes of Manhattan's other famous skyscrapers. I had as much interest in visiting the World Trade Center as I did the Statue of Liberty, and yet one evening I found myself taking the long elevator ride to the top of the North Tower, for reasons I would never have predicted. I was on a date. She and I were headed to Windows on the World, the fancy restaurant occupying the 106th and 107th floors. It wasn't the dinner menu that drew us so high off the ground. It was the dancing.

Swing dancing was all the rage in the late nineties. In summer, large crowds showed up to the plaza at Lincoln Center for their Midsummer Night Swing series. Likewise, this ritzy establishment in the World Trade Center would open itself up to swing dancing on certain nights at no cover charge. I had zero experience but an abundance of false confidence, which allowed me to step, rock, and twirl with my date, in some pantomime of the real thing. On the large dance floor we gasped with exhilaration. Then we gasped again beside the tall, paneled windows with their sky-high view of Brooklyn, lower Manhattan, and the Jersey coastline.

On Sullivan Street, my bedroom fire escape offered a trenched but picturesque view of Washington Square and the backdrop of Midtown. In the evenings I brought out a folding chair and listened to jazz or Chopin's nocturnes (one of the few classical CDs I owned) as I drank tea. One evening I had over an MFA friend and fellow writing instructor, someone who'd quickly become my closest confidant. In spite of that confidence, I still quibbled with her when she asserted that the landmark due north of my fire escape, with its illuminated crown and tall antenna, was the Empire State Building—and *not* the Chrysler Building, as I'd referred to it. She'd lived in New York for a couple of years but came from New Jersey, which gave me enough leeway (hard to believe, in retrospect) to cling to my stubbornness. The matter was settled by a quick phone call to my father, who easily deduced from our location, and my description, that the structure was—and could only have been—the Empire State Building.

That was but one of many discoveries I was constantly making. In the West Village, the narrow lanes and elegant townhouses made you feel like you'd stepped into a quiet London neighborhood. Everywhere you walked, you were tempted off the street by another bookstore. There was the underground Bleecker Street Books, the quaint Three Lives & Company, and the prolifically stocked Unoppressive Non-Imperialist Bargain Books, to name just a few. Those West Village streets remained hostile to the city's up-and-down grid. How easy it was to lose yourself among this weave of diagonality and misdirection, where, against all logic, West 4th Street intersected with West 11th. You'd be lucky to find yourself there. On this beautiful corner stood a tiny French restaurant called Tartine, where you dined in a cozy interior that felt lost to time or sat at one of their small sidewalk tables. Tartine was a place to bring my visiting parents or to splurge, on very rare occasions, with the same grad-school friend who'd corrected me on my fire escape. On an early fall evening, as the pre-darkness spread itself across the Village, my friend and I shifted our plates around to share each other's mussels and steak frites, feeling as well-to-do as any of the well-heeled patrons from around the neighborhood.

In that first semester, it surprised me to learn that Arthur Miller was still alive. My program offered a few free tickets to hear him read at the 92nd Street Y, and I got the jump on one. From the moment he entered the stage that night, I found it impossible to take my eyes off him. He trundled out to the podium shouldering a heavy bag and slightly favoring that same side, looking aged but not old as he spoke with a grandfatherly polish. His voice was crisp and exact, like a metronome. Gracious and remarkably down to earth, the legendary playwright read a piece about his teenage years working at an auto parts supplier on West 65th Street. Without sounding boastful, Miller told his audience that his knowledge about auto parts had far exceeded that of his peers. In that same, even tone, he shared his surprise in learning that no other Jew had ever worked for this company before. This was in the early 1930s, and from a woman in his office he heard about an unspoken resentment among his male coworkers, based on their belief that Jews always stuck together and were helping each other get through the Depression. This was news to Miller, he said jokingly to his audience, as he'd never observed such practices in his own experience. But this "mythology," as Miller called it, gave him an important insight as a young man. Some sixty-plus years later, he reminded his audience that such tribalism was about to cost the world millions of lives, and he warned us, even as we neared the cusp of the twenty-first century, that this pernicious tribalism had yet to be resolved.

That fall, the Yankee great Joe DiMaggio passed away. My father described Joe DiMaggio as smooth in everything he did—from running to hitting to fielding—but to me he was best known for his mention in the Simon and Garfunkel song "Mrs. Robinson." I also knew him as the TV spokesman for Mr. Coffee and—like Arthur Miller—as a onetime husband to Marilyn Monroe. DiMaggio's hitting streak of 56 consecutive games was in no danger of being broken that fall, but another Major League milestone, Roger Maris's single-season homerun record of 61, would be toppled by two different players: Mark McGuire of the Cardinals and Sammy Sosa of the Cubs. On deck was Barry Bonds, who would surpass them both a few years later before all three players were eventually tainted by steroid allegations.

Another historic milestone would be shattered that fall. For only the second time since our nation's founding, the president of the United States was impeached. The event followed a multiyear investigation into a supposedly shady land deal in Whitewater, Arkansas, that preceded Bill Clinton's time in office. After finding no evidence of criminal wrongdoing, Ken Starr, the special prosecutor, shifted his focus to allegations of a sexual liaison between the president and his young intern, Monica Lewinsky. Clinton had denied the affair during a deposition in a separate civil lawsuit, but the discovery of secret recordings and a semen-soiled dress meant that Clinton had perjured himself under oath. It was all the fodder that Starr and congressional Republicans needed, and they jumped on the president with both feet.

As the fate of the impeached president moved to a Senate trial, my own situation hung in the balance. My roommate problems paled in comparison, but my outrage felt no less justified. It wasn't simply the blaring television: It was the food-covered dishes that languished in the sink for days on end, the trail of empty (or half-empty) Coke cans on the counter and floor. When my roommate went out, she would abandon the cordless phone in her unmade bed, only to remind me that it had to be recharged *at all times*. Once, she asked me to turn the TV off—not down, but completely off—on the grounds that her apartment time was more precious than mine, as she worked in an office during the day. If I pointed out her ear-splitting TV habits, or any other inconsistencies, she responded by pouting quietly or, at her worst, slamming the door as she stormed out. The handwriting was on the wall: It was time for me to go.

In mid-December in New York, the days turn dark around 4:30. An upstart wind blows through the city, predicting colder weather that will long outlast the Christmas lights. That winter, I steeled myself for another round of apartment hunting. I stalked the bulletin boards at cafés and around campus, pored through announcements in the *Village Voice*, checked Craigslist and a website called Roommate Finder. What spared me from sinking into disillusionment was a listing I happened upon at NYU's housing office. It was an apartment share on West Houston Street and Sixth Avenue, whose rent—I rubbed my eyes in disbelief—was $530 a month. I went to see it that very day: a proper three-bedroom that was rent-stabilized with an enormous (albeit cluttered) living room, an elevator, and a ground-floor laundry room. My own bedroom was substantially smaller than the other two, but no matter. It had a closet, space enough for a few extra pieces of furniture, and a window that overlooked the building's parking garage and a slice of Houston Street.

My female roommate was a child therapist who worked in a number of Brooklyn schools. The male was a freelance illustrator who often slept during the day, played electric guitar with the sound channeled through headphones, and listened to radio shock jock Howard Stern. Sometime later I would learn that the house he'd grown up in, in Mount Kisco, New York, was used for a scene in the movie *Ragtime*, an adaptation of E.L. Doctorow's novel. Both roommates were older than me by a decade or more, and this provided a brief glimpse into what my life might be like down the road, should I still be living in New York. I tried not to think about it. I had a home in Greenwich Village, a stabilized rent that was beyond compare, and the ability to support myself as I went about the long, slow business of writing.

And I had an amazing roof deck. A few months later, I would learn about the oversized deck that was furnished with benches, Adirondack chairs, and picnic tables. These were set among planters with small trees and a surround of flower boxes with marigolds, baby snapdragons, and English ivy. On the corner of Houston Street and Sixth Avenue, the seventh-story view extended all the way from the West Side to the East Village, and from Midtown down to lower Manhattan. To the north lay the Empire State Building (properly identified) and the elegant stone façade of the Con Edison clock tower; to the east stood the gorgeous beaux arts building that housed the Angelika Film Center, plus a fleet of old water towers that colonized the rooftops of SoHo; to the southeast I could see a sliver of the distant Manhattan Bridge and an array of classic stone skyscrapers that marked the edges of City Hall and the financial district.

As the first warm days of spring arrived, I turned into a frequent visitor of the roof deck. The Twin Towers and the Empire State Building stared at each other like chess pieces across a large playing board. In between lay a motley of shapes and configurations, buildings that owed their existence to the disparate imagination of a thousand architects. In whichever direction you looked, the shades of brick ranged from organic red to tawny yellow to painted hues of pink, white, and pale blue; I saw mansard roofs with shingled dormers and wooden shutters; there were Gothic cathedrals, brownstone churches, and churches of roughly textured fieldstone. It was a comfort to see the city's foundation of brick, stone, and mortar still holding on against the glass towers and ceaseless development that pushed their way in.

After a long work week, my friend who'd grown up on Bleecker Street would escape with his family to their country house in Pennsylvania. An hour-and-a-half car ride would deposit them in a remote, wooded property with a large back lawn that sloped down to a patchy swamp and neighboring creek. They went to one lake for swimming and another to take out their motorboat; in the endless forest behind their house, they went hiking in summer and cross-country skiing in winter. Such getaways were a prized commodity for New Yorkers of means—be it to Fire Island, the Hamptons, or Connecticut. My own retreat was much closer to home, and it was someplace I could visit on a daily basis. Just four flights up from my apartment, a rooftop sanctuary awaited. It was a place I could go to breathe in nature, duck the friction of roommates, and keep at bay the collective pressures that city life was always threatening to impose.

Only a Man

I settled in for the long run. Not just in New York City, but in the hard work of writing. It was a point driven home to me in my spring semester workshop, which coincided with my move to Houston Street. The workshop leader was a comforting figure to us all. Soft-spoken and inherently kind, he set a fatherly, egalitarian tone as he looked for the best in our writing. Each week he made us feel as though our stories mattered—as though the characters we wrote about mattered—even when our work didn't deserve it. At the same time, he tried to realign our career expectations. He read to us an essay by Ted Solotaroff, called "Writing in the Cold: The First 10 Years," in which he highlighted the common experiences of self-doubt, isolation, and anonymity that most writers feel when they're still getting their legs underneath them. Solotaroff very much championed the value of that extended period. It was more important, he believed, to work at your craft under the radar than to fast-track your way to publication and early success. The latter, of course, was precisely what most of us wanted (and what a few of us actually accomplished). But the essay helped sober us up, as did the sense that our workshop leader himself had taken his own sweet time and had only arrived at his position after much hard work and patience.

The desire to *Be a Writer* already made me self-conscious. I never used that term on my own, and I became sheepish whenever friends, or their encouraging parents, stuck that label on me. And yet there was another side of me that, in spite of Solotaroff's advice, hoped for quick publication. It was a longing not simply to see myself in print, but to validate the path I was on. A college friend had already published his poems in a few prestigious literary journals, and one time, when I shared his good news with my father, my dad responded by saying: "That's great, and when are you going to get *your* work published?" I was stunned. His criticism felt slipped in through the back door, and I lashed out defensively. Why was getting published so important, I demanded? In the spirit of Ted Solotaroff, I asked why publication had to be the be-all, end-all. My father shrugged and told me it wasn't. "I've just never known a writer who wasn't published," he said, a truth so casually piercing that it left me with no rebuttal.

My Texas friend had also published an astonishing work of fiction in the *Mid-American Review*. The story was well-honed, professional, and a reminder of how high a bar one needed to set—and how much work it took—to produce that kind of writing. I recalled reading a letter once in which Gustave Flaubert bemoaned the difficulties of his chosen craft. To the poet Louise Colet, he complained that "Writing requires a superhuman will, and I am only a man." At the time, his words had struck me as more than a little melodramatic, but in the years since, they'd begun to ring true in ways I found undeniable.

In my MFA program, I saw writers of great talent who seemed to churn out stories only a few days before submitting them to workshop. I saw thinly disguised memoir trying to pass itself off as fiction. I read about recent college graduates from upper-middle-class backgrounds who were adrift in New York City, characters with dull jobs who were confounded by relationship troubles. The prose was clean and compelling. The narrators had a knack for wry observations and a sardonic take on insolvable problems. The style was in keeping with some of the more celebrated story writers of the day (I won't name them). I recoiled from it. To me it seemed like a shortcut, not to mention egotistical, to hold up a mirror to ourselves so frequently. But who was I to judge? My own stories launched into settings and characters that were far removed from my personal life, yet no one would ever confuse these stories for masterpieces. That was putting it nicely.

So I went the other way. I marinated my work in the dating life of city people, in the awkward social exchanges of college grads, in the professional lives I saw (or imagined) taking shape around me. I likened these to the post-graduate stories of Fitzgerald or the poignant short story "A Little Cloud" by James Joyce. Here was a fiction that seemed quiet yet unsettling. The protagonists were intelligent but fragile, and their epiphanies owned a beautiful self-awareness that was ultimately incapable of saving them. All of a sudden, with this one flip of a switch, my writing felt unrestrained. Brisk sentences flowed from narrators who sprinkled in little notes of irony. I was visited by an invigorating and prolonged head rush. Only afterward, when the feeling inevitably wore off, did I recognize the stories for what they really were. I saw how little depth there was beneath the surface gloss. It wasn't James Joyce or F. Scott Fitzgerald I was reading: It was a bunch of easy tricks and stylized moves like the ones that had repelled me in the first place.

To my previous inroads I returned. I tracked down characters from small towns who lived closer to the landscape and had no professional aspirations. In a craft class for E.L. Doctorow, I wrote a pastiche of *As I Lay Dying*, Faulkner's family drama that continually rotates first-person narrators from chapter to chapter. My own story followed the same pattern of alternating points of view, and the family drama revolved around an escaped cow stuck on a frozen lake after being secretly released by the troubled younger son. Since Faulkner allowed the deceased mother to have her say in one chapter, I gave my fictional cow the same creative license. With pride and belief in the story, I put it in a manila envelope and sent it off to the *Sewanee Review*, convinced that this fabled literary journal from the fabled Southern institution would recognize the story for what it was. Their longtime editor certainly saw enough in it to write me back. On a personally typed postcard, he wrote, "Dear Mr. Liebson: I don't believe that 'Cold Pastoral' works." After a paragraph explanation of the story's many faults, he pointed out one last flaw: "A segment written from the point of view of a marooned cow is all but disastrous."

I was undeterred. The story went out to a number of other literary journals, one of which rewarded me with a complimentary, handwritten letter from the editor in chief. In passing on the story, he suggested, without irony, that I take a look at Faulkner's *As I Lay Dying*.

I continued to send out my work, and the flattering letters continued to accumulate in my desk drawer. In moments of despondency, I would think back on Solotaroff's essay. There was some comfort, if not relief, in hearing him say that "rejection and uncertainty and disappointment are as much a part of the writer's life as snow and cold are of an Eskimo's." And then one day, a surprise stroke of fortune arrived. I won third prize in a student writing competition with the *Atlantic Monthly*. It was accompanied by a check for $250 and a nice letter of recognition by the editor. Not long afterward, an agent reached out with a friendly solicitation, which was forwarded to me through the *Atlantic*. All my previous sobriety flew out the window. No matter that I had only a few finished stories and no novel on the horizon. I stuffed my work into an even larger envelope and sent it along, marked REQUESTED MATERIAL. I felt as though I was finally about to turn the corner, but credit this literary agent for setting me straight. So kind in reaching out to me, so gracious in asking to read my writing, he faded away so quickly and disappeared into the wind.

The world of fiction seemed determined to drag itself out slowly. I stretched my MFA from two years into three (four, counting the preceding one in Ohio). I divided my time between teaching and freelance copyediting. I worked week-long gigs at places like *Allure*, *Arthur Frommer's Budget Travel*, and *Redbook*, or late-night shifts at *Business Week* and *Entertainment Weekly*. Those latter two positions offered free dinners and a car service home—but they also meant getting to bed at one or two in the morning. The work paid well—twenty or even twenty-five dollars an hour—but, unlike teaching, copyediting blocked out extended periods of writing time, or else it left me too exhausted to make use of whatever time I had. Both jobs created their own avenues for burnout. The great thrill of being in the classroom, of discussing handpicked readings by some of my favorite authors, was offset by the toil of grading student homework and essays. The wonky pleasure I took in proofreading magazine copy, in scrutinizing individual sentences for word choice and punctuation, was hard to sustain for eight hours a day, five days a week.

The stress from college students ill-disposed toward feedback could be matched by magazine writers who were just as unwelcoming. There was one movie critic I occasionally feuded with, a writer whose prose, when it fired on all cylinders, was lively, compelling, and very insightful. Sometimes his insights came packaged in a writing that was unnecessarily difficult to follow. Picture a single sentence that was filled with multiple asides—interjections that were set apart by dashes or commas—which would not only stretch out the sentence but force the reader to play hopscotch—to scroll backward and forward to sync up what came earlier with what followed—all while the sentence took on ever more water, until the ship finally reached its landing point. When the sentence worked, it worked. When it didn't, I would apply the red pencil. One night, we got into a heated argument over a sentence so meandering that it would've made William Faulkner proud. Losing my cool, I told him that I had a master's in literature and taught college writing—yet *I* couldn't understand his sentence. If he were that confident that his readers could, then by all means: leave it alone. He stared down at the copy again, took a long moment to himself, and then grudgingly picked up his pen and approved the corrections.

This exchange had taken place well after midnight, and it served as an important reminder. I had to be careful. To invest so much in other people's writing didn't score me extra points or earn me any extra money, but it did risk using up my own reserve of writing capital. The same thing was true of teaching. After finishing my MFA program, I taught a highly enjoyable but intensive ESL course that summer. It was lots of fun but meant lots of prep work, and lots of feedback, and by the time it ended I was grateful not to be teaching again that fall. I came to the decision that, from that point forward, I would have to budget myself. I would take just enough freelance work to pay the bills, and I would preserve that essential "butt-in-chair time," as one workshop leader had called it.

With no more early classes to get up for, and no magazine work to drag me out of bed, I wrote late into the night and would wake up at my own leisure. Such was the case one Tuesday in September, on a summer-like day when I was lazing in bed and not yet attuned to the world, and I would learn that an airplane had crashed into the South Tower of the World Trade Center. What I didn't know then—and what no one could've predicted—was that another airplane was headed for the North Tower, and that the city as we knew it was about to change forever.

PART TWO

Avenue of the Americas

September 11th, 2001

The city, for the first time in its long history, is destructible. A single flight of planes no bigger than a wedge of geese can quickly end this island fantasy, burn the towers, crumble the bridges, turn the underground passages into lethal chambers, cremate the millions.

–E.B. White, "Here Is New York," 1948

I.

THE NEWS ARRIVED AT MY bedroom door by way of my roommate. A genial, gray-haired illustrator who often worked through the night, Mark gave a polite knock as he announced that a plane had crashed into the World Trade Center. It was a little before 9 a.m. The word *plane* implied something small and private: a corporate jet, some kind of puddle jumper—the type of plane your mind would allow to fly off course and collide with such a highly visible obstruction. Mark had assumed the same thing—as had millions of other New Yorkers. The second assumption was that it had been an accident. Of course it had. What kind of pilot would intentionally steer his aircraft into a Manhattan skyscraper? Less than an hour later, we would all learn exactly what kind.

I dressed and ascended to the seventh-floor roof deck—missing, by a matter of moments, the second tower being struck by another jet liner. A number of residents were already assembled by the roof's southern ledge. Our location at Sixth Avenue and Houston Street gave us sweeping views of Greenwich Village and SoHo, whose rooftops hosted their own mini-congregations. Everyone's eyes were trained southward—toward the bottom of Manhattan—where each Twin Tower was marked by a burning gash of several stories. Side by side, these fuming slits bled an endless dark smoke into the morning sky.

Some people were taking pictures, others filmed with small digital cameras. A set of binoculars made its way around the roof. We were roughly a mile and a half from the World Trade Center, but the separation seemed much greater. Few people had even noticed the second airplane. They'd assumed the second blast had been caused by the first building: one giant explosion that reached across to trigger another. All talk centered on the daunting task of repairing these two skyscrapers—which every last one of us expected would still be standing when the smoke cleared.

At my turn with the binoculars, I saw bright shards of glass and drifting debris within the thick billows of smoke. Aimless sheets of paper wafted upward, somehow escaping the blaze. A lone helicopter hovered nearby—not a rescue chopper, it turned out, despite everyone's hopes. Someone remarked that the helicopter was at risk of combustion if it drew too close. All of the sudden a gasp came from the woman next to me. She covered her mouth and pointed a shaky finger, saying she'd seen—or believed she'd seen—somebody jump from one of the towers. No jumper had crossed my binoculars, but with the naked eye it was much easier to imagine the worst of any stick figure shed by the buildings.

Over the next hour a lull set in. People returned to their apartments for television updates, which was what I'd done when I learned of a third plane crash: this one into the Pentagon. At that point, all remaining doubts were put to rest. America was under attack. It was 9:37 a.m., and the FAA ordered all flights—some 4,500—to be grounded. Evacuations began at the Capitol Building and in the West Wing of the White House. I was still processing this news as I headed back up to the roof, where something just as unfathomable had already occurred.

An enormous gray cloud stood in place of the South Tower. Even after a neighbor told me what happened, it still didn't register. I thought he meant several floors had collapsed, or maybe a super large chunk of debris. The amount of smoke was astonishing.

"No," he repeated, "the *building* collapsed. The entire thing came down."

I couldn't imagine what that even looked like. Had the building toppled over as one giant colossus? Did it break apart and fracture into multiple pieces? A demolition-style collapse—like an old casino wired with explosives—didn't seem possible.

What the mind fails to grasp, the eye more easily absorbs. I would learn this lesson a half hour later, by which time most people had returned for good to their apartments or gone to work. The crash of United Flight 93, in a field near Shanksville, Pennsylvania, was still unknown to me at that point, as was the story of its brave passengers who stormed the cockpit and thwarted a likely attack on the Capitol Building or the White House.

I had crossed the street to buy two rolls of film from my corner bodega. This was clearly an historic moment in the making, though it was hard, as I pointed my camera at the one remaining tower, not to feel a pang of voyeurism. The smoke poured out lighter than before, but it was also much denser, like the emission from a smokestack. The flowers on my roof remained in full bloom, offering a poignant contrast to the stricken building, which I tried to capture from a number of different vantage points. I'd begun setting up behind a potted tree when someone shrieked from across the roof deck.

A circular blast exploded from the tower's crown. I saw a giant ring of black smoke—peppered throughout with shining glass—which slid downward in an immense fountain of debris, taking the building with it. I ran from the tree and managed to rattle off a few shots—lightning fast—before it was over. Just like that, the tower was gone. The building had disappeared to leave a massive smokescreen, a mirror image of the one I'd seen a half hour earlier. I stood gaping from the roof deck's edge, still stunned by what I'd just witnessed, when I was shaken again by a terrible thought. What had this looked like to everyone at street level—and what were the consequences to all those people on the ground?

I would find out soon enough. A mountain of footage quickly circulated on television, from split-second images of each plane crash to the prolonged aftermath of each terrifying collapse. One amateur video, shot straight upward from the sidewalk, shows a plane whooshing into the top left corner before vanishing into the South Tower. Three separate blasts erupt—a trident of explosions from the entry point and two nearest sides—while on the far side, barely a second later, nothing more than a single ember shoots through. It's all that's left of the giant aircraft: a small, dying comet that drags behind a thin contrail of smoke.

The buildings rained down with pulverizing rubble and blistering clouds of debris. In one disturbing video, people run straight toward the camera as they flee an approaching tidal wave of smoke. For a moment the camera stares resolutely at what's coming toward it, but soon the frame turns jittery as the cameraman himself starts to backpedal. Out of nowhere, another wall of smoke rounds the corner of a much-closer building—and suddenly the lens loops around as the cameraman begins running in earnest. Facing forward, he captures all the people sprinting up ahead, when he and everyone else come to an abrupt stop. A huge wall of smoke cuts off the path in front of them. It's at least as high as the wall they've been trying to outrun, and here's where the screaming begins. Multiple cries pierce the microphone as a darkening haze envelops the street. "*Oh, Jesus—*" one woman sobs. Her voice comes through a drizzle of falling debris, right before the frame fades to black.

Here's what Pompeii must have been like. Everywhere you turn brings more danger; everyone you see is running for their lives. People panic in ways that are familiar only through movies. On that smoke-darkened street, narrating after the fact, the cameraman describes in voiceover the burning he'd felt in his lungs. "Just relax," he kept repeating to himself. "Don't hyperventilate." But how were you supposed to relax during an apocalypse? One newswoman tried to find out. In a live street report, she walked up to a man whose entire body was covered in plaster-like residue. Weary and shaken, the man looked like he'd stumbled out of a war zone. He'd made a last-second escape from the South Tower, somehow navigating his way to safety, and the reporter asked him to recount what he'd just witnessed.

The man stared wide-eyed as he shook his head at the microphone. "You don't want to know," he told the reporter, before he turned and walked away.

***

The phone lines were jammed all morning. After repeated tries I eventually reached my father at work and my mother at home. The danger felt like it had passed, but my mother insisted I stay home anyway, and when I told her everything would be okay, she got angry. "*Promise* me," she demanded.

Did I ever make that promise to her? More likely I had offered some kind of tactical evasion, an answer that fell short of being a flat-out lie. I knew that nothing on earth could've kept me inside all day.

Few of us had any destination in mind. We took to the streets out of a basic need to be among other people. On Sixth Avenue the wail of sirens was continuous. Ambulances kept ferrying people to hospitals uptown while many of the police cars were caked in dust. Several had their windows blown out. A score of helicopters buzzed overhead, a vigilance that would persist for days to come. The avenue teemed with endless migrants emptying out of lower Manhattan, dust-covered refugees who passed among crowds of restless onlookers. People lined the avenue, packed the rooftops, filled the balconies, and jammed together along the fire escapes. A great curtain of smoke hung over the bottom of the city. At the front edge, the iconic Woolworth Building stood partially concealed by a thick gray shroud that seemed intent on overtaking it.

A peculiar sight jumped out at me. I noticed, set against the chaotic and smoky background, a solitary street sign that read Avenue of the Americas. That was the nickname for Sixth Avenue, and the street sign, dwarfed and alone amid this strange atmosphere, seemed to capture the tragedy of the moment. I tried to fit all these elements into one photograph, but I couldn't decide how wide the shot should be, or how best to line everything up. I was still framing the picture when I happened to spot an old college friend who lived in the neighborhood. For a split second I held the camera in place and considered ignoring her, but then I thought better of it and went over to say hello.

I shared a group hug with her and her boyfriend. We asked each other the same questions everyone else was asking. *Are you okay? Is everyone you know okay? Can you believe what happened? It's just unbelievable...* The dialogue felt as necessary as it was mundane. We asked about fellow classmates who worked in finance, none of whom, so far as we knew, had been in the towers. A nervous energy overtook me. "I think I saw someone jump," I said. "From my roof deck—while everyone was watching. I'm not really sure..." I didn't *want* to be sure, I added quickly, which they both understood. Before parting, we hugged again and said to take care, and then, to my lasting regret, I didn't bother going back for that photograph.

Except for a few vehicles emerging from the attack zone, Sixth Avenue was entirely devoid of traffic. On a short side street, a parked delivery truck had begun to draw a crowd. Pedestrians rubbernecked as they walked past, a few of them stopping outright. I saw a plainclothes policeman on the other side of the truck. He wore an FBI-style windbreaker with a badge hanging from a chain around his neck. Another plainclothes officer came over and whispered to him before the first guy placed a call on his cell phone.

A bizarre and unsettling image was painted across the truck's cargo. It looked like a row of block-shaped steel buildings, all of them windowless and patched with steel panels, in some futuristic city. Each building was a letter, in fact, and together they formed the words Rebel style. Astonishingly, a fighter jet flew just above these buildings, its wings loaded with missiles and the plane surrounded by an explosive orange fire-cloud. The jet's body was also comprised of letters, balloon-shaped and squinched together, which spelled the word KaBoom.

A flurry of questions spread rapidly. Where was the truck's owner? Why had the truck been left unattended, right out in the open? Could this really be just a coincidence—an attack plane threatening what looks like a city—on today of all days? The policemen conferred quietly in their FBI-style windbreakers. They offered little assurance to the growing number of concerned spectators. I didn't see who sounded the alarm, but the words "truck bomb" rippled suddenly through the crowd to ignite a mad scramble. I sprinted at the head of the pack toward Houston Street, and toward the apartment I'd been warned not to leave in the first place.

Of course, the whole thing had been a false alarm. Word got around that it was the work of a gang in Queens, which tagged with graffiti all the vehicles in a local parking lot. To those of us who drifted back, a closer look suggested that the block buildings were a prison, as evidenced by a few threads of razor-wire fencing and a small guard tower. The attack plane might've indicated a form of breakout. This time, I didn't fail to snap a couple of photographs, although later that day, when I spoke to my parents again, I made no mention of the incident. The story of a truck bomb that never was would hardly be vindicating in the eyes of my mother and father, and it could only inspire more fear and dismay in two parents who were already on edge.

II.

On the morning of September 12th, a sky-high white smokescreen continued to hang over lower Manhattan. Fires raged on in the Pentagon, where an estimated eight hundred people had died. My neighborhood felt eerily quiet, as the streets below 14th were closed to traffic. So much ruin lay so close to me, yet the destruction itself remained out of sight, walled off by the tall buildings of the Financial District. Only from the lingering smoke cloud, and the many images on television, could you tell it was there.

The headline story of *The New York Times* described the "merciless sight of bodies helplessly tumbling out" of the burning towers, "some of them in flames." For those who were on the ground, it said that "Every sound was cause for alarm.... People hid beneath cars and each other. Some contemplated jumping into the river."

The first official recorded death was Mychal Fallon Judge, a chaplain with the New York City Fire Department. Just one day earlier, Father Judge had spoken at a memorial service for fallen firefighters. On September 11th, after the first plane hit the South Tower, he rushed to the city's emergency command post, which happened to be in the North Tower lobby. The chaplain offered prayers and comfort to both victims and rescuers alike. It was harrowing, nonstop work. For every smash to the ground they heard, everyone knew it was another person. Even to a seasoned chaplain, the enormity of suffering took its toll. Father Judge reportedly yelled, *"Jesus, please end this right now! God, please end this…* "The distressed chaplain was said to be repeating those words at the very moment when the neighboring tower collapsed. Flying debris rained down suddenly across the lobby. In a matter of seconds, a crushing fragment struck the chaplain's head and instantly cut short his prayers.

All around the city, photos of the missing went up. They were plastered to lampposts, playground fences, and the sides of buildings. Their names were spoken by loved ones, often whimpering, on the local news. We learned that the investment bank Cantor Fitzgerald, occupying four floors of the North Tower, lost 658 of its 960 employees. Every day became a seesaw of emotions. When your eyes didn't sting with grief, your heart swelled with gratitude for the rescue workers and emergency responders. You felt overwhelmed by men who'd run up into the stairwells, not down, in buildings that were drenched with flame. You were overwhelmed by stories like the firefighter who'd been told to evacuate, as the South Tower was deemed unstable, and who'd yelled back into his radio: "I refuse the order."

When you saw the New York Mets and Yankees take the field, wearing baseball caps that read NYPD, NYFD, and PORT AUTHORITY, it was enough to bring you to tears. Same thing when you saw three-hundred-pound football players holding hands during the national anthem, their faces not just wet but streaming. Across the street from me, each time I passed a small pedestrian island, a makeshift memorial brought a lump to my throat. It was more than the village of candles that got to me, more than the handwritten messages accompanied by so many family pictures. It was a newspaper cartoon blown up to poster-size, which depicted a giant fireman and a giant policeman standing together over a smoking Manhattan skyline.

Underneath the image, the caption read simply: NEW YORK'S OTHER TWIN TOWERS.

I was moved, in spite of myself, by the mayor. Rudy Giuliani had been at the emergency command center—the same place as Father Judge—when the South Tower fell. Everyone there had run for their lives, and Giuliani had clearly been shaken by the experience. Walking the streets afterward, this blustery, sometimes-tyrannical mayor seemed transformed into a humble, sympathetic figure. He'd turned into a leader who looked as vulnerable as his constituents: a man who seemed to understand, maybe for the first time ever, the limits of his own power.

***

I had planned to visit my parents that week, but my flight to Chicago, like all other commercial air traffic, was canceled. Even after flights resumed, leaving New York by plane was next to impossible. Renting a car was no easier, but I managed to secure a one-way rental from the Westchester County Airport. So it was that on Monday morning, September 17th, I found myself in one of the many ticket lines at Grand Central Station. It was shortly after 8:30, and a rush of commuters flowed through the Main Concourse. As the line inched forward, I gazed up at the great arched windows with their elegant grids of cast-iron and thought about the Musée d'Orsay in Paris. Did I imagine it then, or was the noise of the station gradually dying down? The noise drained slowly at first, but after a few more seconds the entire Main Concourse had gone quiet.

I turned around to see a space open up in the middle of the enormous hall. The sea of commuters parted magically, and through the lane of spectators came twelve firemen, traveling in two columns of six each. They wore their dark protective gear with reflective yellow stripes, keeping their eyes straight ahead as though unaware of the attention. What started as a modest rumble of applause quickly built into a loud ovation. It swept the ground level of the Main Concourse, ascended the lofty marble stairwells, and echoed throughout the massive hall. Still the men carried on without breaking stride. Where could they possibly be going? What mission could've brought them to the heart of Grand Central Station on that Monday morning? None of us knew—and none of us dared to find out. You would no sooner stop these men than interrupt soldiers on a field of battle. Only six days removed from September 11th, a dozen firefighters had tried to pass unnoticed through one of the busiest hubs in all of Manhattan, but a thousand New Yorkers refused to allow it.

The next morning, after my 2 a.m. arrival at my parents' house, I awoke early to attend Rosh Hashanah services. I hadn't been to synagogue in many years, and the High Holidays felt weightier than they ever had. Something simmered in the pained looks people traded outside Beth Emet, in the hushed comments people gave each other before going inside. I successfully avoided my old Sunday School classmates, but I was forced to speak when my mother introduced me to her acquaintances. "He's visiting from *New York*," she told them, with special emphasis, until I finally asked her to stop.

I'd looked forward to hearing from my childhood rabbi, a man of great warmth and solemn benevolence, but the morning service would be led by a female rabbi he now shared time with. Credit this young woman for her spunk. Beth Emet referred to itself as "The Free Synagogue," founded on a principle of "free speech from the pulpit," and this rabbi took that notion to heart. She didn't whitewash what many in the congregation were feeling. The old Hebrew God was accountable, she seemed to be saying, as she told us we had every right to be angry. But the rabbi didn't forget her job either, and she reminded us, no matter how upset we were, of our continued obligation to pray.

From the prayer book *Gates of Repentance*, the rabbi asked—and the congregation answered—the elusive question that had plagued our people for millennia:

When will redemption come?
When we master the violence that fills our world.

There was a beautiful simplicity to those words. And yet how quickly they came unraveled. What did mastering this violence actually look like? Did it mean stamping out those who would commit violence against us, or did it oblige us to gain control of our own violent impulses? In my journal I burned up several paragraphs on the subject. I vented about holy men who massacred innocents, men who lay in hiding like crocodiles to ambush their prey. Elsewhere, I expressed skepticism about my own hunger for retribution, a desire that much of the country shared. It was our nature, as Americans, to require some overseas explosions at least as large as the ones over here.

So it came to pass. On October 7th, the United States and Britain launched air and missile strikes on al-Qaeda and Taliban targets in Afghanistan. Once more, all eyes became glued to the television. The giddiness of battle was quickly followed by aftershocks of fear, as Americans were warned about sleeper terrorist cells that may have already dug in. Before the first bombs were even dropped, envelopes containing anthrax spores arrived at several news organizations in New York and Florida, plus the offices of two US senators. New York governor George

Pataki had to evacuate his Midtown office when anthrax spores were found in the building. My father prescribed me a bottle of Cipro, the antibiotic to treat anthrax exposure, and for many months the vial of pills sat atop my dresser in the hope of going unused.

I determined not to be paranoid. I wasn't going to change my life or let myself be upended by fear. And yet a modest fear still gnawed at me whenever I descended the subway stairs, set foot in public parks and movie theaters, or happened to pass through Times Square. In Penn Station, it was hard not to be spooked by men in paramilitary outfits leading around bomb-sniffing dogs. It was the new reality we all shared. That reality meant having to take off your shoes and unpack your laptops in airport security lines. If your bottle of contact solution was over a certain size, a TSA agent would confiscate it, or if you'd mistakenly brought your nail clippers—as I did for my return flight from Chicago—an agent would hastily remove them, snap off the pointed nail file, and return the disabled weapon to your carry-on.

III.

For several years after September 11th, I watched the annual name-reading ceremony on television. Two members from different families shared a podium and alternated reciting from a batch of names, at the end of which the camera would swing to two new readers at a separate podium. A quiet strain of violin music played in the background. For the last two names in every group, each reader would state the name of their own relative, often with their voice quavering, as they added a personal, loving remark. One mother, bursting into sobs, called her son the light of her life, and her heartache brought you right back to the terrible day itself, and the immense pain that had consumed the city for so long.

At the firehouse on Sixth Avenue and Houston Street, home to Engine Company 24 and Ladder Company 5, I attended the yearly moments of silence. The backed-out fire trucks blocked a lane of Sixth Avenue while the men lined up in the mouth of the garage, wearing their dress uniforms. For the first anniversary, over a hundred bystanders turned out. There were parents with young children, dog walkers, men with overcoats and briefcases; one teacher led a troop of well-behaved students. Greeting cards and colorful bouquets filled the entrance and lined the sidewalk in front of the station. The number of onlookers consistently dwindled over the years, to the point where only a few people stood watch as the next generation of firemen bowed their heads.

In 2014, the city fulfilled its promise to rebuild. A tapering, octagonal glass structure—the so-called "Freedom Tower"—dwarfs all buildings in lower Manhattan. A far more interesting piece of architecture sits behind it. Two square pools, nearly an acre each and thirty feet deep, occupy the footprints of the former towers. At the top of each pool, the surrounding parapets shoot out thin jets of water from hundreds of finger holes, which together form a beautiful threaded curtain on each of the four sides. Down below, the pooling water drains slowly toward a square void in the center, from which the water disperses to parts unknown. "Reflecting Absence" is the name of the artist's original design, and even a brief visit to these memorial pools makes any other concept impossible to imagine.

From my one visit, I've kept a permanent souvenir. The victims' names are engraved across the eight bronze parapets and grouped by category—first responders, flight victims, and so forth. As I wandered around both pools, I didn't bother to consult the legend. I preferred to read the names randomly, hoping that some individual might jump out at me: some personal story might jog my memory. It seemed like a long shot, but I was lucky, as I turned one corner of the south pool, to spot the name of someone whose story I knew quite well. I quickly unfurled the rectangular white cloth the memorial had provided. I spread the fabric swatch over the embossed letters and began rubbing with a black crayon, also provided by the memorial. I worked the crayon back and forth along the fabric—moving it left and right, up and down, over and across each letter—until the name MYCHAL F. JUDGE had fully imprinted itself.

That swatch of cloth still sits in my closet. It's a reminder of so much sacrifice and so much selflessness in a time of despair. It's a reminder of the final speech delivered by Mychal Judge himself, just one day before the Twin Towers fell. On September 10th, the day before his own life would be brutally taken, Father Judge stood before an audience of firefighters and told them: "We have to hold each other for as long as we have each other." By these words, the beloved chaplain lay down a marker for an entire grieving nation to follow, and he exhibited a faith that could light the candles in any house of worship across the land.

E.L. Doctorow and The Writer in the Family

When I was sixteen years old, my father surprised me one night with a knock on my bedroom door. He lingered in the hallway a moment, staring at a worn paperback that he turned back and forth in his hands, before he finally presented it to me. "Here, I thought you might like this," he said. I saw the words *Loon Lake* printed across the front cover. The author—E.L. Doctorow—was no one I'd heard of, though the name certainly sounded like that of a writer. "He reminds me of you," my father said. "The young man in the book, there's something about him that makes me think of you." He shrugged, perhaps a little embarrassed, and allowed me to accept or reject the offer.

Of course I accepted it. This was a rare, surprising flash of intimacy from my father. He was a cardiologist who spent long hours at the hospital and routinely missed out on my Little League games and wrestling matches. The fact that he considered me enough to make such a comparison—even to a fictional character—was an acknowledgment I found deeply moving.

No matter that my life barely resembled that of Doctorow's protagonist. Joe of Paterson is a hardscrabble young man who cheats, fights, cons a living, flees his New Jersey home for a brief stint in New York City, then finds his way to an industrialist's secluded resort in the Adirondacks. The setting is one of beautiful women, gangsters, and forlorn poets. It is also a place where Joe's dreams begin to merge with his reality. Though *Loon Lake* doesn't dwell very long in Manhattan, Doctorow's writing about the city still lingers for me. Joe describes New York in the days before glass-and-steel high-rises dominated the skyline: "It had size it had magnitude, it gave life magnitude it was one of the great cities of the world. And it went on, it was colossal, miles of streets of grand famous stores and miles of streetcar tracks, great ships bassoing in the harbor and gulls gliding lazily over the docks."

Whatever my father saw of me in this character, I saw my dad's own image reflected in this young man. My father had no greater passion—and showed no quicker nostalgia—than for the New York City of his childhood. In moments only semi-related, his mind would hook on some totem of his youthful days, and next thing he'd be recounting stories about the city's elevated subway lines, its former baseball players, what movies he'd seen in which movie houses, what famous buildings and landmarks he'd visited—and exactly how old he'd been for each occasion. Animated by memory, his words would take on a stream of consciousness that matched both the tone, and enthusiasm, of Doctorow's protagonist.

I found *Loon Lake* to be a stirring novel, albeit with several bumps along the way. The book shifts point of view relentlessly, offers cryptic flashbacks, even contains long passages of verse. And yet the story always circles back to Joe of Paterson: the resilient young man who bears himself—by his wits, and by his instincts—through an increasingly suspenseful plot. After finishing Doctorow's novel, I would hurry through several more of his books over the next few years: *Billy Bathgate*, *Ragtime*, *World's Fair*, *Welcome to Hard Times*, *The Waterworks*, and *Lives of the Poets*. It was in this last book—a novella and short stories—that I read what would become my favorite work of short fiction: "The Writer in the Family."

The story takes place in 1950s New York, where a teenage boy (coincidentally named Jonathan) has recently lost his father, Jack. To spare his grandmother the tragic news, Jonathan's Aunt Frances makes up a story about his family moving to Arizona, and she enlists her nephew to write letters describing their new life in the desert. Jonathan obliges her. He talks about the unexpected beauty of the barren landscape, the great health benefits of the dry air, and the bright future he sees for himself—all in the voice of his deceased father. The authenticity moves his aunt to tears. "You're so right," she exclaims by telephone: "he loved to go places, he loved life, he loved everything."

Each time I reread that passage, I tear up as well. Part of this is due to Aunt Frances, whose reaction makes it forgivable—or nearly forgivable—that she would demand such a letter in the first place. But the real clincher lies with Jonathan himself. Incredibly, while still mourning with the rest of his family, he somehow pulls it off. Jonathan looks back on his father's life in New York City—on all the exciting discoveries his dad used to make, all the gifts he'd return with from distant neighborhoods (from "ships chandlers" to "foreign vegetables")—and out of these memories he constructs a living portrait on the page. Long before I'd ever read Doctorow's story, I already anticipated a similar role for myself. I imagined the day would come when I sifted through my father's past, arranged his life into a meaningful narrative, and tried to perpetuate his voice after he was gone.

By the time I read that story, I'd already formed a strong connection to the author. Doctorow provided a point of contact between me and my father, an attachment made deeper by the many similarities shared between both men. These included New York City childhoods at roughly the same time (Doctorow was born in 1931, my father in 1936); family backgrounds that consisted, at least in part, of Jewish immigrants on the Lower East Side; a public education in the outer boroughs (Bronx High School of Science and Forest Hills High School, respectively); and—encapsulating all of the above—an abiding interest in the history, lore, and intriguing public figures of New York. This last point was evident in much of Doctorow's writing, which portrays a romantic sweep of the city in an era that bleeds into my father's own awakening in New York.

The novel that most captures that awakening is *World's Fair.* On the original jacket cover, a pair of mysterious geometric shapes—one round, one triangular—tower before a drawing of the city skyline. Those strange figures, which resemble Egyptian hieroglyphs, are as emblematic of my father's childhood as anything else. They are the Trylon and Perisphere. They are the two icons of the 1939 exhibition in New York City. My father described them longingly while I was growing up, and he later wrote about them in an essay called "Cityscapes," for the Chicago Literary Club. Almost sixty years after the event itself, my father reminisced about his wondrous visit to Flushing Meadows, Queens:

> *A generation after the Great War, I was fortunate enough to see the City of the Future. One of my early memories was of the World of Tomorrow....*

> *The theme center, a 700-foot-high tapered triangular pylon, and a 200-foot-high perisphere, symbolized representations of infinity.... One ascended to the perisphere by a series of long escalators and most were seated above a large panorama of the city of 1960 by day and by night. Highways were ribbons of perfection, the city provided "an electric assurance of a better life."*

He'd been three years old at the time. Of the remarkable ascent he took—to the top of an extraordinary structure with a magnificent view of the future—my father would lament that, "to many who experienced it, it has never been matched."

That sentence came as no surprise to me. Long had I perceived some crucial part of his life was anchored to that moment. The tug of his past had never really slackened, and I knew that whatever else unfolded for him, it would never live up to the glowing promise held out to him at such a tender age.

The novel *World's Fair* parallels the story "The Writer in the Family" in many ways, from the family composition and Bronx neighborhood to the father's past in the Navy and as a failed music-store owner. In the novel, however, the father is still alive, while the boy feels like a younger version of Jonathan. He's given the name Edgar—Doctorow's first name—just as the other characters take their names from the author's real-life family. (In a 1986 *Paris Review* interview, Doctorow refutes any autobiographical claims by saying the book only "pretends" to be a memoir.) The novel is a quiet story told mostly through Edgar's observations, plus occasional narrative asides by other characters, about the family's day-to-day life during the Great Depression. Two dramatic moments stand out. The first is when Edgar gets confronted by a couple of large bullies on the street, who accuse him at knife point of being Jewish. Edgar firmly denies it, lies about his father being a cop, and afterward is left to live down his shame.

The second scene is when Edgar goes under the actual knife—during emergency surgery—after a burst appendix. As the doctors put him under the gas, he fights kicking and screaming with the fury of someone being waterboarded. In recovery afterward, still under the effects of anesthesia, he floats through a dream sequence in which he's visited by his deceased grandmother. The old woman cools his forehead with a damp washcloth and offers him a penny from her pocketbook. Then she tells him—in a Yiddish he somehow understands—that he's a good boy and that God would protect him.

Just like Jonathan, Edgar turns out to be the writer in the family. He enters an essay contest with the World's Fair—on the subject of how to define a Typical American Boy—and wins honorable mention. His name appears in the newspaper, and he receives free passes to the fair for his entire family. His greatest reward, however, may come when his father recites the essay aloud in the living room. Edgar is touched by the depth of feeling in his dad's voice. He cherishes the gloss of approval it confers on him. The essay pays tribute to the economic sacrifices of his mother and father, and it states that an American boy not only "cooperates with his parents" but "knows the value of a dollar." If the boy is Jewish, Edgar asserts, "he should say so." Such a boy, Edgar concludes, "looks death in the face."

The essay makes his mother cry, while his father draws out his handkerchief—and how could the reader not succumb as well? But Edgar's dad has one more gift to give. As he consoles his son for not winning first prize, he states what the reader has already figured out long ago: that Edgar is "not a typical American boy and that's all there is to it."

***

Beyond the similarities between Doctorow and my father, I also felt a kinship with Jonathan's dad in "The Writer in the Family." Certain details in his life don't correlate with my father's, of course. A store owner turned appliance jobber, Jonathan's dad never made "the great journey from the working class to the professional class"; nor did he follow his well-married sister to the suburbs of Westchester. My own father, on the other hand, joined the ranks of the medical profession and eventually left New York City for the northern suburbs of Chicago. Thankfully, their fates also diverged over the premature death of Jonathan's dad. Even in that respect, however, an interesting parallel exists. Jack floats through Doctorow's story as a relatively distant figure, someone defined more by his absence than his proximity to his family. Only through snippets of memory does he get revealed, especially as Jonathan tries to compose each letter. His son recalls a man who never traveled but loved New York unceasingly; a man of great vigor who "moved with a bounce," "always wanted us to go someplace," and "was always eager to see what was around the corner."

In my own father, who was often remote and difficult to access, lay the same kind of excitable attitude. He spent most nights secluded in his bedroom study, where he did work from the hospital, lost himself in his reading, or memorized old baseball statistics for the umpteenth time. At family gatherings he lacked the stamina for long interactions, and in social settings he invariably turned inward and retreated to a more comfortable solitude.

And yet, at a moment's notice, he would spring forth from isolation and go looking for company. I'd hear him humming from the top-floor bedroom, and next thing his footsteps took to the staircase with a resounding gait—*one*-two, *one*-two. A nimble energy flowed from him. He was a shorter man who rarely exercised, yet he owned the strongest grip of anyone I knew. Even during my years as a wrestler, his handshake would overpower mine. His hands featured in a favorite game of his, where he held his palm face-up and encouraged me and my brother to slap him as hard as we could. "*Harder*—" he'd command, after one of us went. We took turns striking him—using bigger and bigger wind-ups—to no effect. "*Harder!*" he'd repeat, pretending to grow impatient. By then my own palm had turned red. My fingers were throbbing with pain. Finally, my brother and I changed tactics. After a giant windmill we slowed our hand down at the very last second—right before contact—and offered his palm the softest, feathery touch. "*Owww!*" he screamed. His hand jerked away as if scalded by a hot poker. He waved it in the air and blew on his fingers like they were still on fire. My brother and I burst out laughing. After shaking the pain away he brought his palm back in front of him, like a pupil ready to receive his next punishment.

If his devotion to the past sometimes put him on an island, it also infused our lives with stories, gags, and amusements. On Sundays, as our parents dismantled the *New York Times* and *Chicago Tribune*, the kids went straight for the funnies. Whenever my father saw *Dick Tracy*, he would reliably fall into a favorite impression from childhood: Fiorello La Guardia. During the 1945 delivery-truck strike, Mayor La Guardia went on the radio to read the funny papers to deprived families. "Ahhh, here's Dick *Tra*-cy," he announced, as he came upon the comic detective. My father pinched his mouth in imitation and gave his voice the lilt of an old-fashioned newsreel. At the end of the strip, the mayor—as impersonated by my father—demanded of his young audience: "And what does it all *mean-n-n*, children?" My father stretched out certain syllables for added effect. "It means that *Dir*-ty *Mon*-ey never *Brings* any *luck*!"

If I sassed him as a kid, he would often sass me right back: "Don't talk, chum. Chew Topps gum." It was a famous advertisement of his day. If we were out driving and he spotted an antique car, he would break into song: "*He had to get UN–der, get out and get UN–der,... to fix his oh-old machine.*" It was the spry, silly chorus of a 1913 tune about a man whose automobile kept breaking down. If one of us saw the antique first and started singing, my father's voice would quickly overtake ours, spreading an infectious glee through the car. Years later, I discovered the actual lyrics were somewhat different. They went: "*He'd* have *to get under, get out and get under, to fix his* little *machine.*" I also learned that a popular version had been performed by a singer named Bill Murray—an amazing coincidence, as the well-known actor with the same name hailed from my hometown.

A few years after reading my father's "Cityscapes" essay, I entered NYU's creative writing program. With E.L. Doctorow on the faculty, it was impossible not to imagine him meeting my father one day. I envisioned these men with similar pasts and common interests hitting it off like old friends. My own meeting with Doctorow would have to wait. By then he'd become more of an elder statesman to the program, teaching an occasional craft class and supervising a few master's theses, but no longer leading fiction workshops. Add to that the sabbatical he was on, and it wouldn't be until the spring of my second year that we finally landed in the same classroom. Thus began my semester-long effort to make him a mentor—and hopefully bring my father along for the experience.

Doctorow wore round spectacles, had a trim gray mustache and jawline beard, and combed his remaining threads of hair over his crown. His eyebrows were his chief means of expression. Sometimes they would furrow with skepticism or arch ironically; other times they split farther apart with confusion or disbelief. A dry smile softened the effect. On opening day, he boasted that the writers on his syllabus all possessed a single attribute: what he called a "fevered imagination." Some of the headliners were Heinrich von Kleist, Edgar Allen Poe, Flannery O'Connor, Virginia Woolf, and—to everyone's surprise, in a craft class on fiction—Dante.

Unfortunately, the fever he alluded to spiked less frequently in the room. The majority of group time belonged to student presentations, a number of which left something to be desired. And yet every so often he would interrupt the presenter to ask a pointed question or, even better, to chime in with his own thoughts. It was in these moments, as his gaze turned from the student speaker to the students at large, that the room grew alert and we all sat up straighter in our chairs.

Almost by accident, it seemed, he would disembark from his place of silence and slip into the role of raconteur. Doctorow's voice was hushed but mellifluent. With the natural fluctuations of a storyteller, it would climb in scale and then drop down to a low, throaty pitch. Many of his tales he'd told previously at readings or in interviews, but no matter. We'd all signed up to hear the great writer speak, and we eagerly snatched up whatever-sized morsel he threw our way. One favorite anecdote involved a profile he'd written for a high school journalism class—on a doorman from Carnegie Hall who, as I recall, was a survivor of World War II and Nazi Germany. His teacher found the piece so moving that she insisted on inviting the man to class. Doctorow deflected, saying the man was a recluse who preferred his solitude, but when his teacher wouldn't relent he finally came clean. The man didn't exist: Doctorow had made the whole thing up. (His grade—he also admitted to us—had subsequently been lowered.)

The author spoke candidly about his own frustrations with writing and his many stare-downs with failure. This included one dark moment when he'd been so disgusted with the early draft of a novel that he threw the whole thing away. The book was based on Julius and Ethel Rosenberg—convicted Soviet spies and former front-page tabloid news—and he told himself that if he could make *that* story seem dull, then he had no business being a writer. Into the trash can he chucked those pages, and in a fit of anger he began pounding out a parody of his own work. It was the best thing he could've done. What began as an exercise in self-mockery would eventually lead him to the very voice he'd need to make the novel work. That voice belonged to the son of his fictionalized spies, and so *The Book of Daniel* was born.

The point of this, and his other anecdotes, was to underscore the importance of the imagination. Once ignited, it would liberate the writer and disperse his story in unforeseen directions. Doctorow said that every novel he'd ever written had been born by a creative accident. They had begun, more precisely, by what he called "a private excitation of the mind." *A private excitation of the mind!* What writer wouldn't want that.

As an example, he offered none other than *Loon Lake.* He'd seen those two words on a passing road sign while driving through the Adirondacks, and as they rolled around mysteriously inside his head, he began to envision a private train traveling through those same woods, only fifty years earlier. The train, he realized, was on its way to a lavish retreat owned by some wealthy industrialist: a man who took up with various mobsters and beautiful women. The author put one of those women aboard his train, made her visible to a young man observing from the woods, and from there he rode the rails all the way to the end of his novel.

What I didn't obtain from Doctorow in class, I sought instead through office visits. Based on our mutual interest in Sherwood Anderson and William Faulkner, on the many overlaps between him and my father, and on the many books of his I'd read, I persuaded myself that I'd earned an extra share of his attention. The author received me cordially enough. When I appeared at his door he seemed genuinely interested, but he didn't unlock any hidden drawers for me or provide any deeper access to his personality. Nor did he dole out any extra confidences in response to my own. I shared with him, for instance, what I took to be an astounding coincidence: On the same night that he read a passage from his novel *City of God*—a flashback encompassing both World Wars and that involved a pilot parachuting into a boneyard in France—my father presented a talk at the Chicago Literary Club on three British war poets (Wilfred Owen, Siegfried Sassoon, and Robert Graves). The parallel didn't seem to register as powerfully for Doctorow. Later, when I brought a first-edition *World's Fair* to be signed for my father, I didn't expect him to remember that particular story I'd recounted, but it saddened me that in inscribing the book, he made no reference to the 1939 exposition they'd both attended—and which had made such a lasting impression on both their lives.

It was the same disappointment when I brought him a first-edition *Lives of the Poets*. This time the inscription was for myself, and I very nearly asked if he would sign it: "To Jonathan Liebson, the writer in the family." But I wasn't sure I'd earned that title yet, and part of me wanted his comment to be self-generated: a personal token based on our many discussions. It was not to be. Doctorow inscribed the book, To Jonathan Liebson, NYU alum, All Best—and in that moment I realized how unrealistic my expectations had been all along. I'd aspired to build a three-way bridge between Doctorow, myself, and the man who'd introduced me to his work, somehow believing it would strengthen the bonds between father and son. Instead, I had only briefly entered—and would soon fall out of—the author's orbit, while the bonds I'd anticipated would remain what they had always been: a private excitation of my own mind.

And yet I still had Doctorow's writing. In the years after finishing the program, I turned away from his newer novels but went on reading his earlier books. At the same time, I continued to teach my favorite short story to my undergraduate classes. Whenever it came back into rotation I would mention the story to my father, who perked up momentarily, affirmed his memory of it, and expressed his affinity for Doctorow. To this day he still does, though the conversation has lost the steam of our previous talks—and it never touches on the origins of our shared connection to the author.

Several years later, on a fall afternoon when I was teaching at The New School, I spotted Doctorow near a small post office on West 10th Street and Sixth Avenue. From a few doors down I instinctively raised my arm to say hello, but he didn't see me—and something prevented me from calling his name out. Perhaps I believed the man deserved his privacy, but another side of me feared he might not remember who I was.

The scene in which Aunt Frances cries, after reading Jonathan's first letter, still brings me to tears. So, too, does the story's remarkable ending. By then, Jonathan seems stuck in an unwinnable feud between his mother and Aunt Frances. His mom resents the lie of Arizona, just as she resents the obligations still being imposed on her late husband. "He can't even die when he wants to!" she yells in protest, which makes Jonathan's task ever more difficult. What's perfectly obvious to her, to Jonathan's older brother, and to every last one of my students, is the way Jonathan has let Aunt Frances manipulate him. It was she who dubbed him "the writer in the family"—a note of praise that came with a hefty price tag, as his aunt convinced him that unless he wrote the letters she wanted, he would bring dishonor upon himself and his father's memory.

Fortunately, Jonathan wises up by story's end. In his final letter to his grandmother, speaking as his father one last time, he not only breaks the news of his dad's terminal illness, but he calls the move to Arizona a mistake. This may be the story's most profound insight. Jonathan writes: "As for the nature of my ailment, I know that I am simply dying of the wrong life." The words are a subtle jab at his Aunt Frances, while they acknowledge, on his father's behalf, a man so beholden to the wishes of everyone else that he never got to fulfill his own.

And who else, besides Jonathan, is capable of laying his father to rest? Who else looks beyond Jack's business failures, financial setbacks, and economic shortcomings to reveal what truly mattered to him? Thanks to Jonathan, we see a man who thrilled at everyday discoveries; a man who noticed the rare and exotic where most others never bothered to look; and a lifelong New Yorker who loved his city with a passion that never relented. In the end, what started as a burden for Jonathan turned out to be a blessing in disguise. The letters transformed him into the most authentic version of what a writer should be: someone who not only describes but inhabits the very individual he's trying to portray. For those of us still hoping to understand our fathers, can there be any reward more profound?

Café Culture and Celebrity Sightings

If you threw a rock in a New York City café, how many writers would you hit? Ask any writer and they'll quickly tell you the answer: too many.

They are like creatures at a watering hole. They prefer to go about their business unnoticed, even as they constantly pay attention to their surroundings. Who among them is a potential competitor? Who among them is a potential threat? Which of their fellow patrons are secretly working on the next big screenplay, novel, or self-help masterpiece?—and what is it they're drinking?

In New York City, cafés drive a local economy of artists, novelists, screenwriters, journalists, students, professors, and the like. These public spaces are a friendly alternative to the library or home office, as you can burrow in for long stretches of time without feeling like a monk. Most places have free Wi-Fi, coffee refills are but a few steps away, and you can always take a break to people-watch. While few cafés are pin-drop quiet, most provide a tolerable level of ambient noise, and in the louder ones you can usually get by with a pair of headphones.

Cafés are where I go to write in my journal, to prep for class, to grade student essays, or to hand-mark printed drafts of my own writing. For many years I would read the *New York Times* sports section cover to cover, until the habit consumed so much of my time that I finally, reluctantly, had to drop it. My other indulgence was the *Village Voice*: the progressive weekly founded in the 1950s by Norman Mailer. When it hit the red plastic bins each Wednesday, I would snag a fresh edition off the top of the stack, duck into a café, and flip straight to the movie section in back. The writing was highly descriptive, always energetic, and often padded with tall vocabulary words. I took as much pleasure in their snarky critiques of big Hollywood blockbusters as I did their more thoughtful reviews of low-budget films. Among city publications, the *Voice* carried the most comprehensive listing of independent theaters, film festivals, and foreign features. Sadly, after continually slimming down over the years, the print edition finally became a casualty of the digital age.

A close friend from college likes to romanticize my café lifestyle. He grew up on Bleecker Street in its more bohemian days, attended LaGuardia High School of Music & Art and Performing Arts (the school on which the movie and TV show *Fame* are based), and, in spite of becoming a radiologist, still maintains an artistic predilection. He enjoys portraying me as a starving writer who spends all his time in coffee shops, a depiction I probably get too defensive about. The image suggests an ethereal, carefree existence that contradicts the dull reality in which I spend far more time alone at a desk, revising uncooperative sentences. But—to be fair—I, too, share a romantic view of cafés. I indulge in the belief that on any given day, some chance encounter might inspire or elevate me: some random meeting might alter the course of that afternoon, that week, or maybe even the trajectory of who I am.

This has occurred multiple times. The first was at a popular Village café called the Grey Dog, which I discovered shortly after moving to New York. The hangout remains on Carmine Street, though it moved, after a brief absence, just down the block. (It also opened several other locations over the years.) In its original spot, an extended bench connected the side tables along two exposed brick walls, while up front a few tables huddled before the tall, retractable windows, which in summer folded up like Japanese screens. The iced hazelnut coffee made me swoon. The thin, crispy-edged fries were best devoured with mustard or mayonnaise. In its early years, the Grey Dog not only allowed canines but provided treats and dishes of water. The owners were happy to pay whatever fines the city levied against them, until the officials cracked down hard enough that the owners finally relented.

Not long after the impeachment of Bill Clinton, I began to see his former intern—the one he'd claimed not to have had sexual relations with—at the Grey Dog. Monica Lewinsky had been subjected to unwarranted smear campaigns on television and in the press, courtesy of those who blamed her for undermining the president. I myself was a big Clinton supporter, but it was obvious that this very impressionable, very young woman had suffered at the hands of those who were far more powerful than her. That included not only the president but his opponents, who used her as a pawn in their own impeachment scheme. Monica fled the bright spotlight of the nation's capital for the relative calm of Greenwich Village, where a brief interaction provided me with a humorous anecdote I've enjoyed sharing ever since.

Everyone at the Grey Dog treated her kindly. The owners and staff called her by her first name, and in my experience the other regulars always left her in peace. I did likewise, though I couldn't resist sneaking a peek at her from time to time. Twice, that I was aware of, she returned the favor. One time, I was fairly certain she threw an appraising glance at an out-of-town friend of mine. Another time, on a day when my allergies were acting up, she turned to me at the end of a sneezing fit and offered the polite, customary reply. From that day forward, I began telling people—with a straight face, and with perfect irony—that I had been blessed by Monica Lewinsky.

In New York City, it is an unwritten rule that you grant celebrities their privacy while, for their part, they avoid drawing extra attention to themselves. Most of the time, both parties abide by these rules. At the now-defunct café Grounded, on Jane Street in the West Village, I would sometimes spot a well-known writer and TV personality who kept his head down and maintained a low profile, even though his poofed-up curly locks identified him almost as readily as Kramer from *Seinfeld*. I managed to restrain myself in his company, in spite of the childhood smart-ass that still lived inside me and snuck out on occasion. At a place called Once Upon a Tart, on Sullivan Street in SoHo, that old urge almost got the better of me. While waiting in line one day, I stood behind a retired tennis player whom I'd seen for years on television. In my mind the man resembled Clark Kent, of the Christopher Reeve era, with the same prominent cheek bones and cleft chin—though his blondish-red hair distinguished him from the Man of Steel. This was in the middle of May, the spring weather had begun to shift toward summer, and I gathered myself to say, "So, do you miss Paris this time of year?"

No doubt he would've gotten the reference. This former number one player, who wore a baseball cap and hit punishing ground strokes, was a two-time winner of the French Open:

the Grand Slam tournament played on red clay just outside the City of Light. As he spoke with the barista about his plans to move, and how much he would miss the neighborhood, I grew itchy waiting to pop the question. Experience had taught me that I only had a brief window of time to address a stranger—famous or not—in a way that felt natural, before the words started to sound rehearsed or risked coming out like a line. By the time they'd finished their chat, that window had unfortunately closed. Sadly, the tennis player and I would never cross paths again, but over the years I continued holding that same question in the back of my mind, on the slim chance I ever bumped into Rafael Nadal ordering an espresso.

On another occasion, at the Doma Café on Perry Street, it took every ounce of willpower to keep my mouth shut. A short man with a dwindling fringe of hair sat at the center table, where he held forth so loudly that he seemed to be demanding everyone's attention. He had a distinctly nasal, slightly chirping theatrical voice—which you'd easily recognize if you'd ever seen the movie *The Princess Bride*. In that picture, the actor repeats the line "Inconceivable!" multiple times, to the point where it marks him like a verbal tattoo. What was inconceivable—to me—was the way this actor expressed himself so brazenly in such a public setting. Perhaps because I'd always associated him with his small role in the movie *Manhattan*, and no doubt because he and the director share the same physical stature, I nearly stood up and yelled: "Hey, Woody—could you keep it down already!"

***

If you walk up Sixth Avenue through the heart of Greenwich Village, turn left at the corner of Waverly Place—site of the historic Waverly Diner—you will arrive, within a short half block, at the marvelous three-way intersection of Waverly and Gay Street. This narrow lane of brick townhouses and white-washed apartments feels like an alleyway to another time period: a preserved corridor of the early nineteenth century. On the near corner resides a small coffee shop with broad, ceiling-high windows and two benches stationed out front. Depending on which table you get, you'll have a view of one, the other, or both of these magnificent streets.

Originally named Joe The Art of Coffee, now called Joe Coffee Company, and always referred to as "Joe's" by its regulars, it's the kind of place where frequent customers tend to pick each other out and form a distant curiosity, even if they never act on it. One day, one such regular gave me an extra-long look from across the café. It was the kind of stare that exceeded ordinary politeness. As soon as I noticed him taking notice of me, he stood from his chair and walked right up to my table. The guy had a sharper eye than I did. It turned out we both lived in the same building, though only he had realized it. That was but one of our many coincidences, which included a shared Midwestern childhood (Ohio and Illinois), a background in French from small liberal arts colleges, a short-lived past as public-school French teachers, and freelance work as copyeditors. This screenwriter and I were also city cyclists, and it would become a habit, whenever one of us rode past a new café, to send along a scouting report to the other. I'm certain that at some point—either through the laundry room or the building's roof deck—he and I would've become acquainted, but I've no doubt that our friendship developed more quickly, and became that much stronger, thanks to our mutual interest in cafés.

There was another fellow I saw fairly regularly at Joe's. He had disheveled black hair, a black goatee, and thin black glasses that clearly marked him—as did the perpetual stack of papers on his table—as an academic. Those papers could've been his dissertation or student essays: I didn't know because we never had a full-on conversation; we only exchanged a few pleasantries here and there. Over the years we continued to see each other—the guy was always grading or rewriting—until at some point the café got so popular that the wait time for a seat made it prohibitive. I ended up taking a hiatus for a few years, and wouldn't you know that the next time I wandered through its doors, the guy was still there. Except that this time, he wasn't sitting at his usual table—and he wasn't sitting by himself. Little did I suspect it, but this guy was about to enter my life in the most amazing and unpredictable of ways.

Sometimes there's an uneasy friction between patrons and café owners. Artists and grad students can linger for hours without blowing through their limited income, while proprietors, though welcoming of all customers, are still in the business of—well—staying in business. To encourage turnover, the Grey Dog would dispatch a roving staff member to keep watch for empty cups and plates. As soon as one turned up, so would the staff member. "Can I clear this for you?" they'd inquire, with a creeping hand already reaching for the item. It was smart psychology. The sight of a dirty dish gave you permission to loiter; it was proof you'd paid your way, whereas an empty tabletop made you more self-conscious and pegged you as a freeloader, even if you technically weren't. The next tactic they used was to dim the lights in the afternoon and set out small candles, which made reading far more difficult and signaled a switch to the dinner crowd. The last—and least subtle—form of messaging came in a painted sign that appeared one day beside the front counter, and which read: NO CAMPING AT TABLES.

I rarely bring my laptop to cafés, but for many years I took up valuable real estate with the *Times* sports section. I would spread it before me like a tablecloth, and, in the same way people consumed tabloids, I ate up every story about scandal, adversity, and misbehavior. I couldn't get enough of it. There were cyclists caught doping in the Tour de France, struggling coaches on the hot seat, spoiled superstars embroiled in controversy, and at least one New York team that was miserably underperforming. It took me many years, and many lost hours of work, to finally kick the habit. Well before then, my addiction to sports nearly ruined me in another spectacular way.

It happened on a winter afternoon at the Grey Dog. The sun was shrinking fast, the house lights were strategically lowered, and I hunched close to the newspaper, stubbornly refusing to take the hint. I moved the tiny candle around like a chess piece, shifting its weak glow from column to column. My eyes trained on the newsprint in front of me when a burst of light threw me back against the wall. "Holy shit—" I blurted, as a sleeve of flame rode up the paper's edge. I leapt from the bench and made a dash for the exit, carefully holding the paper at arm's length, lucky that no one blocked my path through the narrow front foyer. Once outside, I threw the paper down and did a war dance on the sidewalk until I'd stamped out the flames. Seconds later, a woman approached me and asked, serious as can be, if I could please tell her how to get to Caliente Cab. I studied her a long moment. Had she somehow missed the public scene I'd just made, or was she simply indifferent to it? I pointed her toward Bleecker Street and explained how to reach the touristy restaurant at the corner of Seventh Avenue, which no respectable New Yorker ever went near. I tossed the charred paper into a nearby trash can, ducked back into the front foyer, and entered the Grey Dog to a sudden round of applause. My surprise changed quickly to embarrassment, and I avoided all eye contact as I slinked back to my table, where I decided that from that day forward, I would never again disobey house rules.

In the early 2000s, as cell phones swept the city, so, too, did a radical change in people's behavior. Conversations once held in rear payphones suddenly migrated into the main room, as these devices persuaded people that every call was a priority—simply because that call had reached them wherever they happened to be. Diners, shoppers, and customers quickly forgot they were in a public setting—or conveniently forgot the meaning of the word "public." In restaurants and cafés, you would be startled by a lone voice that rose suddenly above its surroundings: a strange, one-way dialogue like something out of a play. No doubt I was overly sensitive to this behavior. If the person was near me I would make an up-and-down motion with my hand, like patting a dog on the head, and ask if they didn't mind speaking lower. Most people obliged and even offered an apology. Every so often, however, someone would hold the phone away and glare at me with a look best translated as, "Who the fuck are you?"

At the Dean & Deluca on University Place, one loud talker proved especially troublesome. The guy sat directly behind me, making it impossible to send him a subtle glance of annoyance. My only option was the full-on, movie-theater-style head turn, which I desperately hoped to avoid. After several more minutes of enduring his conversation, I finally broke. I rotated my entire chair around—subtlety be damned—and felt a chill of recognition as his eyes locked with mine. It was "Paulie," the famous mafia don from Martin Scorsese's hit film *Goodfellas*. That is, it was the actor who portrayed him, but for anyone who's seen that picture, you would forever associate this actor with that role. In the middle of Dean & Deluca, this burly mob boss went right on talking as he stared at me—or stared straight through me—while he plugged his opposite ear with his free hand. I don't recall how long our staring contest lasted, but he finally gave a flick of the eyes and turned his head away, bringing his voice down to a whisper. Suffice it to say that on that day, my sense of pride was only exceeded by my inflated sense of personal bravery.

In SoHo, on an industrial side street tucked between Broadway and Lafayette, not far from the landmark Puck Building and the old BP gas station, sits a rare treasure. Head down Crosby Street for a half block south of Houston, and keep your eyes peeled for the narrow, unassuming entrance to the Housing Works Bookstore. The double doors stand a short staircase above the cobblestones, and behind its easy-to-miss storefront lies a remarkable two-story interior. Picture the private library of a Carnegie or a Rockefeller, and you'll have some idea. Inside the Used Book Café (the store's original name, which I continue to use), a second-floor gallery wraps the front half of the hall, reached by two curving staircases with large wooden banisters. Upstairs and downstairs, hefty wooden bookcases line the walls, and in the back café sit multiple tables for browsing or snacking. At night, the space hosts readings, discussions, and the wildly popular series "The Moth," in which individuals tell bizarre, often unbelievable stories from personal experience, at the end of which the standing-room crowd votes on a winner.

Another favorite venue, which I discovered shortly after moving here—and whose closure still gives me a twinge of remorse—was the café at Cinema Classics. Back in the early 2000s, before Netflix came along, video stores still dotted much of the city, and this combination café and video rental on 11th Street in the East Village also operated a small screening room in back. Roughly two dozen folding chairs were set up on ascending rows of wooden planks, like a carved-out section of bleachers, which faced a movie screen the size of something from a high school classroom. Nobody cared how small the screen was, or the middling quality of the video projection—not with a five-dollar admission fee (later raised to $5.50). In the few years that the place remained open, I saw such pictures as *Rebel Without a Cause, Silence of the Lambs, Rear Window, Miller's Crossing* (my favorite Coen Brothers film), *Annie Hall,* and French movies like *The Grand Illusion* and *The 400 Blows.*

***

One afternoon at Joe's, on a beautiful spring day when I'd scored a coveted corner table, a strikingly attractive woman sat down next to me. She pulled her chair out and lowered herself as casually as a leaf falls onto the sidewalk. I felt my heart skip several beats. Then it went into overdrive. The woman had picked a chair facing the wall—rather than facing out into the café—and with good reason. Here was a star as big as they came. The actress with straight brown hair and lovely dark eyes had gotten an early start in her film career, and by the time she came of age in a trio of unfortunate *Star Wars* reboots, a whole legion of Jewish men had developed a crush on her.

I was one of them. Even in New York, and even after all the luminaries I'd seen or crossed paths with, this one threw me for a loop. My proximity to her was unimaginable. A strange giddiness overtook me, and fearing that a nervous laughter might erupt at any moment, I fled to the bathroom and hid myself away for several minutes. When my nerves had finally resettled, and I'd regained control of my face, I returned to discover a young man sharing her table. It was no accident. The two of them were discussing a screenplay—his screenplay, I gathered—and when I heard him mention his MFA degree from The New School, I jumped at the sudden opening. Excusing myself politely, I told him that I taught classes at The New School and was curious to hear about his experience there. Of course, my undergraduate classes had nothing in common with The New School's MFA program, but no matter. I was happy to engage this young man while making occasional eye contact with his companion, just as you would to any third party in a conversation.

I'd like to report that I eventually engaged my target as well, but of course she was way too clever for that. Each time I looked in her direction, the actress offered me a cordial nod and a faint smile, but she didn't add a single drop to the conversation. By sheer coincidence, I'd brought with me a book of poems by a famous poet who'd taught at the famous university she'd attended, but even that had no pull. Having run out of cards to play, I excused myself again and left the two of them alone, accepting, with a heavy heart, that Natalie Portman and I were simply not meant to be.

Some things *are* meant to be. Some café encounters prove that serendipity is very much alive and well. Take the screenwriting friend from my old building. A few years earlier, we had both witnessed 9/11 from the same roof deck, and yet we'd remained anonymous to each other until the day we finally spoke at Joe's. Since then, he'd become one of my closest companions. Several years later, Joe's would be the site of another inspirational meeting. This one occurred in my first return visit after taking a long hiatus. No sooner had I walked through the door than I spotted the same guy from the old days: that scholarly fellow with the goatee, black glasses, and disheveled black hair. Except that this time around, rather than sitting at his usual table and working on his usual stack of papers, he sat at a different location and was talking to a woman. What choice did I have? I walked right over and butted in to say hello.

I should add that this woman was a friend of mine. She was someone I'd known through my years of freelance copyediting, and yet for some reason she turned bashful when I approached her. Her reception was lukewarm at best, and I soon discovered that she and this fellow, though gabbing like old acquaintances, were actually on a first date. They'd met through an online dating site, and Joe's was the place they'd chosen for their initial rendezvous. I couldn't get over the coincidence. I began peppering the guy with excited questions. Yes, he told me, he had recognized me as well. He was in academics, of course—doing a master's in education—but years before he had indeed been working on a PhD (in philosophy). The guy was easygoing, extremely good-natured, and no stranger to irony—the same qualities that my friend possessed—and so it happened that a year later, on the exact same date, the two of them would marry in a civil ceremony at City Hall. The wedding took place on a beautiful spring day, after which the guests accompanied the bride and groom in a lovely procession across the Brooklyn Bridge. The whole thing felt like a fairy tale. It was a scene that came right out of the movies, so naturally, as soon as I got home, I went straight to my favorite café, ordered myself a large cup of coffee, and wrote about it in my journal.

The following two lists, while not validating my friend's opinion about my café lifestyle, do confirm how much time I've spent in coffee shops over the years. Each place mentioned is one I've been to at least a handful of times. Some of them are still going strong; others—I'm sorry to say—exist only in memory.

In downtown Manhattan:

Le Gamin Cafe, on MacDougal Street; Les Deux Gamins (same owners), on Bedford Street (later renamed Café Henri); Lotus Cafe, on Clinton Street below Houston; Once Upon a Tart, on Sullivan Street; Dean & Deluca, on University Place; Esperanto Cafe, on MacDougal; Café Angelique, on Bleecker and Grove; Mona Lisa Cafe, on Christopher Street; Barnes & Noble third floor café, Union Square; Doma Café, on Perry Street; McNally Jackson (formerly McNally Robinson) Bookstore café, on Prince Street; Think Coffee, three locations: Mercer Street, Bowery and Bleecker Streets, and Eighth Avenue just below 14th; Space Untitled, on Greene Street; Joe's Coffee: one on Waverly Place, one on East 13th; Kudo Beans, First Avenue and East 3rd Street (later reopened under new owners, as The Bean); The Bean (same owners), on Sixth Avenue and 10th Street, plus Broadway and East 12th; Cafe Pick Me Up, on Avenue A and East 9th; 11th Street Café, in the far West Village; Cuppa Cuppa, on East 4th Street; Jack's, on West 10th Street; 'sNice, on Eighth Avenue and West 4th, plus Sullivan Street below Houston; Amy's Bread, on Bleecker and Leroy; Grounded, on Jane Street; Gizzi's, on 8th Street; 88 Orchard, on the Lower East Side (later called Irving Farm); 71 Irving Place, in Gramercy (also renamed Irving Farm); Local, on Sullivan Street; City Girl Café, on Thompson Street; Whynot Coffee, corner of Gay Street and Christopher; Cafe Arí, Greenwich Avenue and Christopher; Corrado Bread & Pastry, Christopher Street and Waverly Place; Third Rail Coffee, on Sullivan and West 4th; Bee's Knees, West 10th behind Jefferson Market Library; Prodigy Coffee, on Carmine Street (near the location of the original Grey Dog); Grey Dog, University Place; Starbucks, three locations: West 4th and Washington Square East, Houston Street and West Broadway, Spring Street and Crosby;

Vagabond Cafe, on Cornelia Street; Rebel Coffee, on Eighth Avenue near West 12th; Fresco Gelateria, on Second Avenue near East 9th Street; and, on St. Mark's Place in the East Village, a tea parlor that deserves honorary mention: Sympathy for the Kettle.

In Brooklyn:

Vineapple, on Pineapple Street; Tazza, two locations: Henry Street and Atlantic Avenue, and on Clark Street; Konditori, on Smith Street; Cafe Pedlar, on Court Street; Le Pain Quotidien (which a friend calls LPQ), on Montague Street; also on Montague Street: Connecticut Muffin and Starbucks; One Girl Cookies: on Dean Street, and the much larger location on Main Street, in Dumbo; Hungry Ghost Coffee, on Fulton Street and South Oxford; Primrose Café, on Greene Avenue in Clinton Hill; Henry's Local, on Henry Street; Bien Cuit, on Smith; Absolute Coffee, on Atlantic Avenue; Swallow Cafe, on Atlantic Avenue and Clinton; Amy's Bread (same owners as in Manhattan), in the same location on Henry Street as the now-closed Tazza; Tekoá, Clinton Street at Cobble Hill Park; Espresso Me, Atlantic Avenue and Hicks; and Joe's Coffee, on the corner of Hicks and Pineapple.

A Run for Obama

In September, New York enters what many consider to be its best season. The oppressive heat of summer flattens out, the warm days grow liberated from the cloying humidity, and the cool nights yield to brisk, pleasant mornings. Even in October, as the afternoons shrink and a deepening chill sets in, the trees entice you with their first few fingers of yellow. It's a sign of more brilliant colors soon to arrive—a promise I'm rarely seduced by. As a survivor of one too many Chicago winters, I'm unable to see autumn as some romantic glide path to the next season. And yet I have, after so many years of living in New York, at least come to appreciate a few delights served up along the way.

In the fall of 2007, summer's end brought its yearly avalanche of course prep. That meant nailing down dates on the syllabus, making photocopies, and taking care of other administrative chores. In the midst of this work, I was informed by my dentist that two of my wisdom teeth would need to be removed. The news was shocking enough to someone well beyond his teenage years, but I was even more alarmed to learn what the extraction entailed. In the era of cell phones, laptops, and laser surgery, the procedure had barely evolved since the dawn of dentistry. The best description is also the simplest: An oral surgeon sticks a pair of pliers in your mouth, latches on to the tooth in question, and yanks his arms back and forth like someone wrenching a stubborn nail from a piece of plywood. Anesthesia blocked the pain, but I felt every bit of that extraction. Even with my hands bracing the armrests, I was still pummeled about in the chair. It reminded me of the short story "The Use of Force," by William Carlos Williams, in which an obstinate young boy refuses a life-saving shot and is eventually manhandled by the doctor, for the boy's own good. Afterward, my oral surgeon held out his palm and showed me one of my orphaned teeth, remarking on how strong the bone was and how well splayed the roots. I felt a strange pride mix with a twinge of regret, having given up that small, nicely sculpted portion of myself.

By late September, with my stitches out and a return to solid food, I was motivated for a much-needed run. It was one of those beautiful, early fall days that everyone raves about. From my apartment I ran due east along Houston Street to the East River, turned left and shot up to 10th Street, then crisscrossed my way back through the East Village. I took whichever side streets the green lights favored, and on that particular afternoon they led me across Broadway at West 3rd Street. Here was an unflattering stretch of modern NYU buildings: a sprawling, Soviet-style housing complex on one side; a row of boxy megaliths on the other. At LaGuardia Place I hit a sudden roadblock. Metal barricades, blue sawhorses, and numerous police officers lined the intersection, while throngs of people were making their way toward Washington Square Park. At first the disruption annoyed me, as I had to choose between doubling back or fighting through the crowd. Then it dawned on me what everyone was doing there. I'd heard murmurings about the event on the radio that morning, and I felt myself suddenly drawn by this mass migration, like an insect to the spell of giant floodlights.

One block north, Washington Square was teeming with spectators and ever more policemen. Among the clotted pathways and congested lawns, I wrangled a few steps here, a couple more steps there, before I couldn't go any further. People waved royal blue banners that said OBAMA '08. Above his name, a stenciled horizon in red-and-white stripes was crested by a rising sun. The afternoon sky edged closer to dusk, and across the park I saw yellow rectangles of light in the townhouse windows. At the foot of the great stone arch stood a makeshift stage, whose platform was too low to grant me and others on the periphery a view of the speaker.

Three years earlier, that speaker had been a little-known state senator from Illinois. His fortunes changed overnight when he gave a riveting speech at the Democratic National Convention in North Carolina. Barack Obama rejected the politicos and pundits who divided up Americans into liberals and conservatives, into red states and blue states, as he embraced instead a *United* States in which everyone belonged to a single American family. Since that remarkable performance, the skinny young man had become junior senator from Illinois, and now, only two years later, he'd decided to launch a presidential bid.

Obama was a rare and undeniable talent. His intelligence, charisma, and good looks put people in mind of the previous Democrat to hold the White House: Bill Clinton. There were a few key differences, however. For starters, Clinton had held much more experience when he'd chosen to run—as a successful governor, and as head of the National Governors Association. Second, Clinton hailed from a Southern state, and no Democrat since John F. Kennedy had won the presidency without Southern roots. In case those factors weren't daunting enough, the young man from Chicago had one more notable distinction: He was Black.

The sky grew darker above Washington Square Park. The canopy of trees fell deeper into shade while the great stone arch, modeled after the famous arch in Paris, stood fully illuminated. A sea of heads angled toward it. All around me I saw hundreds of arms raised like periscopes above the crowd. Some pointed digital cameras or recorders; others held up glowing flip phones like BIC lighters at a concert. Later reports would estimate twenty thousand people in attendance.

At times, Obama addressed his audience like a grand orator. Other times, he displayed the wry satire of a seasoned comedian. His appeal for affordable healthcare, student debt relief, and an end to the war in Iraq drew loud approval from his audience. "Tell 'em, Barack!" someone shouted from the field. I cheered and applauded like everyone else, but the candidate had yet to win me over. The thorny question remained: Was America ready for a Black president? In my heart I wanted to believe so, but in my head I just couldn't be sure. Then Obama took his speech in another direction. He dropped the political rhetoric and employed one of the oldest tools known to man: He told us a story.

The episode he spoke of had taken place on the campaign trail a few weeks earlier. After ten straight days of pounding the pavement, Obama was functioning on little sleep, he sorely missed his family, and he'd just received a scathing write-up in the *New York Times*. Desperate to return home, he still had one last stop to make in rural South Carolina. So on a glum morning, he and his staff trekked out to a remote small town where they were greeted, to the dismay of his whole crew, by a whopping twenty people. The state legislator who'd promised to endorse him wasn't even there, due to a scheduling error. Swallowing his frustration, Obama put on his best game face and prepared to address the crowd, if that were the right word for such a small turnout.

Just then, a tiny old woman stepped forward and beat him to it. "Fire it up," she said to the sprinkling of bystanders, who echoed her words in response. "Ready to go," she said next, and the small audience once again followed her lead. Obama and his staff looked around with confusion. Was this woman a heckler? Should they let her continue or try to usher her away discreetly? The old woman never gave them the chance. Each time she renewed her call—*Fire it up! Ready to go!*—she was met by louder and louder replies from her audience. The drill picked up a quick head of steam, the woman's energy became infectious, and soon Obama and his staff joined in as well. Everyone shouted at the top of their lungs, and the moment gave a surprising jolt to the beleaguered candidate. For the rest of that day, he and his team would erupt at each other with that same spirited battle cry, and for many days afterward they would go on breathing the old woman's fumes.

Didn't we all have some picture of her in our mind's eye? Weeks later, in the heart of New York City, Obama repeated that call-and-response to an audience of some twenty thousand. *Fire it up! Ready to go!* The combined chanting rose above Washington Square, the moment built toward a crescendo, but the climax was still to come. Obama told us that if one small woman could change a crowd, then one single person could change a room. One single voice could change a city. One single person could change a country. And any single one of us could help change the world.

His voice reached a climbing, husky pitch. More than once it came close to cracking. As I added my own voice to the cheering crowd, it struck me that some signs were simply too powerful to overlook. I had stumbled by accident on this extraordinary event, led by an extraordinary candidate in a park named after our country's first president—and how could I refuse what fate, or the workings of my own heart, were so clearly communicating?

On October 8th, it reached eighty degrees in New York City. People wore summer outfits and packed the sidewalk tables, seemingly unconcerned by the anomalous weather or the message from the previous year's film *An Inconvenient Truth*. In that feature-length documentary, former vice president Al Gore had warned of a worldwide catastrophe due to global warming. In New York City, things were about to get even hotter. At the National Book Awards ceremony in November, I watched in astonishment as a public feud broke out at The New School's Tishman Auditorium. After poetry finalist Robert Hass denounced George W. Bush and the catastrophic war in Iraq, Christopher Hitchens, a finalist in nonfiction, took the stage to offer a sharp rebuttal of his "good friend." He defended both the war itself and the toppling of Saddam Hussein. To a growing chorus of boos, he railed in tones that were increasingly dogmatic, an ugly scene that became a perverse moment for Hitchens. The writer seemed unaware of his near-religious fanaticism on display, which resembled the kind that he himself had so frequently criticized—including in the very book that was up for an award that evening.

The heated exchange reflected an ever-increasing divide in our country. As the war in Iraq entered its fifth year, that divide would haunt Hillary Clinton, Obama's opponent for the Democratic nomination. Years before, the senator from New York had voted to authorize the use of military force, but in light of the war's staggering casualties and destabilization of the Middle East, she refused to give a straight answer to a basic question: Did she regret casting her previous vote? Her nuanced replies and highly parsed language drove her supporters crazy, and it drove them in growing numbers toward her opponent.

The calendar flipped to 2008, and the two candidates traded initial primary results. Obama won the Iowa caucuses while Hillary Clinton took the New Hampshire primary and then prevailed in three of the next four contests. On deck was Super Tuesday, when the Democrats held twenty-three primaries across the country. After all the ballots had been counted, both sides could declare victory. Hillary Clinton won the popular vote, but of the nearly 1,700 delegates up for grabs, Obama edged her out by just over a dozen. He'd proven that he could not only stand toe to toe with the towering favorite, but he might even be able to knock her off her perch.

A few weeks later, in a seemingly unrelated sidenote, an ugly glass high-rise took to the air a few blocks south of my apartment. Its construction was one I'd protested the year before, with members of a downtown preservation society, as the monstrous tower seemed almost contemptuous of the SoHo neighborhood in which it would stand. The developer had a long history of dubious real estate deals, and he'd even boasted—after the fall of the Twin Towers—that he now owned the tallest building in Manhattan (a statement contrary to fact and common decency). Years later, that same man would become Obama's loudest critic and chief advocate of the "birtherism" movement: a campaign that falsely portrayed Obama as a non-native US citizen. The bigoted crusade made its ringleader a darling of the right, and it would help propel him, a few years down the line, to the Republican nomination for president.

By early June, the delegate battle was decided in Obama's favor, but Hillary Clinton wouldn't readily concede. She continued to tout herself as the more viable candidate, having won the overall popular vote, an argument that was undercut by one key factor: lingering questions about her likability. The subject had come up during one of the debates, in which Obama, when asked about it by the moderator, responded with uncharacteristic rudeness. Offering a curt, almost grudging, reply, he answered that his opponent was "likable enough."

Summer temperatures rose throughout the Northeast. The radio reported a 94-degree day that felt like 97, and I took a weekend trip to Boston to see an old friend who was hosting a pool party for his two daughters. While he and I sat poolside, sipping beers from our deck chairs, the girls splashed around like porpoises in life vests. My friend told me a funny story from earlier that summer, when he'd invited his older daughter to bring her kite to the beach. Her response had caught him by surprise. How could she fly her kite at the beach, she'd asked, when there weren't any trees there? My friend didn't understand her, so his daughter, all of four years old, explained that you needed to have trees in order to make the wind. "No kidding," I said. I found that answer deeply moving, just as I could tell that my friend had. Wasn't there something beautifully innocent about her observation? We took for granted that the wind made the treetops shake and flutter, but wasn't the reverse just as logical? To a young child who made soap bubbles by twirling her toy wand, or who spread waves in the pool by flapping her arms, wasn't it just as reasonable to believe that physical objects brought invisible forces into the world?

At the end of August, Barack Obama was officially declared his party's nominee. The ceremony took place not at the regular convention hall but in Denver's Mile High Stadium, before a crowd of seventy thousand people. Just a few weeks later, both the Chicago Cubs and the Chicago White Sox—the two baseball teams from the candidate's hometown—would make it to the postseason: a feat not seen in over a hundred years. For the New York Yankees, the season would also end on a historic note. The team played their final game in the original Yankee stadium, built in 1923, as they were moving to a shiny new venue with luxury skyboxes and higher ticket prices. Before the curtain came down, Derek Jeter, the team's stalwart captain, surpassed Joe DiMaggio for all-time hits in the old building, a record no Yankee would ever have the chance to break.

Long before that stadium met with the wrecking ball, the entire US economy was almost leveled. Nearly a month before the election, a crash in the housing market led to a cratering of the stock market, which together initiated The Great Recession. People were defaulting in mass on their risky "subprime" mortgages, which they couldn't afford and should never have been sold in the first place. Investment banks had bought and bundled these mortgages into securities, and as the failing mortgages sent those securities into a nosedive, entire pensions were wiped out, municipalities fell into hardship, and banks and insurers were overleveraged with bad assets. Panic spread of an economic collapse. Companies like Goldman Sachs, which were deemed "too big to fail," received generous government bailouts, while everyday Americans lost their homes and were allowed to go bankrupt. Remarkably, after the insurance company AIG took billions in assistance, executives rewarded themselves with a weekend spa retreat at the cost of half a million dollars.

Amid this financial meltdown, Republican candidate John McCain briefly suspended his campaign. He said he would focus all his attention on his senatorial duties to help the economy. It was a bold move that ended up backfiring. Barack Obama stayed in the race while still serving as senator, making him appear more capable of multitasking than his opponent. His lead climbed to double digits, even as attack ads tried linking him to a former agitator with the Weather Underground, a Vietnam-era group that once advocated for bombing national targets. The lead held up in spite of attacks tying Obama to an inflammatory Black pastor named Jeremiah Wright, whose Chicago parish Obama had attended. The hope was that blue-collar voters would overlook their economic woes out of fear of a radical Black candidate, a cynical ploy that had failed to persuade a majority of Americans.

Election night began auspiciously. Obama won Pennsylvania early, and somewhere around nine or ten on the East Coast, Fox News called Ohio for him. Soon New Mexico fell into place. Then came Florida and Virginia, and by 10:30 Obama was declared the winner. Revelers hit the streets of New York City. Gleeful supporters danced and sang in Times Square. From his ranch in Arizona, John McCain made an eloquent concession speech. The longtime senator and former POW called this a special moment in America's history, and he expressed his gratitude at having been part of it.

Shortly after midnight, Obama took the stage in Chicago's Grant Park. The cold November night couldn't chill the crowd of one hundred thousand, who greeted the president-elect with chants of "Yes We Can." Echoing his opponent, Obama appealed to a larger sense of unity and history. He reminded his audience about a great former president from the State of Illinois—Abraham Lincoln—who had actually been a Republican. And in a sign of how far our country had come since then, he told the story of a 106-year-old Black woman, only one generation removed from the Civil War, who'd lived through the women's suffrage movement, the protests at Montgomery, and the moon landing—a woman who had put her fingers to an electronic touchscreen in the year 2008 and voted for the country's first-ever African-American president.

Still buzzing from the speech, I discovered a voicemail from the college friend I'd celebrated Bill Clinton's victory with, way back when we were recent graduates living in Paris. In my return message, I can't remember if I mentioned that lucky encounter I'd had with Obama in Washington Square Park. I'm pretty sure I didn't bring up that feisty old woman from South Carolina, and I'm positive I didn't say a word about that pool party from the previous summer. The story about my friend's daughter had stuck with me, however. Her words felt strangely relevant to the election that had just come to pass. Wasn't there some prophecy in his daughter's observation? Sometimes we require a more innocent perspective to free us from our everyday assumptions, and to challenge the limits of what we consider possible in this world. Credit the young child for believing a tree can create its own weather. Credit the young candidate for believing he can stir the winds of his country's imagination. And credit all the rest of us for permitting those winds to carry us away.

Confessions of a Cyclist

Sixth Avenue, also known as Avenue of the Americas, starts in lower Manhattan as a modest offshoot of the busier Church Street. Within a few blocks, the three-lane artery quickly fills with taxis and trucks that come piping through SoHo, roaring into Greenwich Village, and racing uptown as fast as the streetlights allow. Amid this frenetic activity, you'll sometimes spot a lone figure on two wheels. Head down, torso bent low over the handlebars, he slips between cars like a nimble fish among a school of sharks. Meet the bicycle messenger. His disregard for traffic is so brazenly absolute that he either rides with a death wish or has somehow discovered the rare secret to invulnerability.

Countless times I have ridden a bicycle up Sixth Avenue, but never once have I braved its central rapids. Even when pedaling alongside traffic, the sense of being expendable is never far from one's mind. Such awareness was lodged in me many years ago, and it has stuck ever since. I'd been riding along the left-hand side and was nearing the intersection with Greenwich Avenue when a snub-nose delivery truck shot past me on my right—then darted left like a bull out of its chute. If I hadn't pumped the brakes *right then*, the vehicle would've sheared me off my bicycle and pulled me under.

Afterward, watching from the curb, I felt a quivering in my arms and legs. It was the kind of feeling you'd expect from a near collision with a multi-ton steel object. The truck itself hadn't missed a beat. It drove along Greenwich Avenue for another block, until the light at West 10th brought it to a halt. A second wave of adrenaline washed over me. My hands retook the handlebars, my feet shoved off the curb, and I was suddenly pedaling at top speed to catch up.

I reached him on the other side of 10th Street, where my hand gave a loud—and not unpainful—smack against the rear cabin. The truck stopped cold. Out popped this burly fellow with a shaved head, shoulders like bedposts, and a Jesus tattoo covering his enormous right bicep.

"What the fuck's your problem?"

I dismounted my bicycle and parked it on the sidewalk. "You almost ran me over," I said. "I could've been *killed*."

Even if my voice hadn't cracked, why did I think such information would chasten him? The guy was no doubt well acquainted with his own recklessness. He came a step closer, at which point he promised that if I ever touched his truck again, he *would* kill me.

"Oh, really," I said, and gestured at his arm. "Is that what Jesus would do?"

Ripples of attention fanned down the block. Lunchtime patrons filled the outdoor tables on both sides of Greenwich Avenue, and what was it—other than toxic stupidity—that held me in place? The man's arms clenched at his sides. His biceps swelled into grapefruits, and as he edged ever closer, my stubborn feet refused to work in reverse. A sudden hand startled me from behind. I turned around right as someone corralled me by the shoulders. "Come on," said the stranger, "it's not worth it." He began towing me away, and I was too stunned to do or say anything. So was the truck driver, apparently, for he made no move to follow. I completely forgot my bicycle as the guy marched me down the sidewalk and out of harm's way. Then this stranger—this guardian angel of a man—set me free. With a pat on the shoulder and a friendly nod, he said, "Just let it go," and then he disappeared as quickly as he'd arrived. In the years to come, I would continue to think about those parting words. *Just let it go*. Was there any advice more urgent—or more challenging to an embattled cyclist?

In New York City, cyclists often feel like scapegoats. Taxis and buses regard you as pests. Parked cars open their doors in your path like booby traps. Pedestrians converge in front of you just as soon as the last car has driven through the intersection. To non-cyclists, I often joke that riding a bicycle in New York is a lot like playing a video game. The surrounding scenery keeps shifting, obstacles appear willy-nilly, persistent mayhem rears its head. The main distinction, of course, is that a quarter buys you multiple lives in a video game, whereas the street affords you but one.

Other people hold a contrary view. Allan Ripp, writing in the *New York Observer*, argues that cyclists themselves are the true nemesis. In a colorful rendition of his own demise, he describes the scenario in which he is "laid out by a bicycle, likely one delivering dinner to one of my neighbors.... There will be just enough time to register the breath-stealing collision that pounds me head-first into the street, with the smell of Teriyaki beef hitting my nostrils."

Is it wrong for me to feel hungry after this description?

In all fairness to Ripp, he is not entirely off-target. Bicycle deliverymen are nearly as treacherous to the city as they are invaluable. Therein lies the rub. For as many New Yorkers who are appalled by these speed demons, there are just as many who couldn't live without them. My own attitude lies somewhere in the middle. Whenever one of these guys (in my experience, they're always men) whips past me in electric silence, I'm at first startled—then deeply annoyed. Their passing feels like a brushback pitch in baseball. Other times, observing them from afar, it's almost impossible not to admire them. Just look at everything they have to endure. In rainstorms they ride around in full-body slickers, like flying tarps racing down the street. In freezing weather they keep their hands in bulky mittens, like giant space gloves cinched to the handlebars. One part of me sees these guys and thinks: "Damn them!" Another part of me can't help thinking: "*Damn*, look at them."

Pedestrians hate cyclists. Cyclists hate jaywalkers. Both groups despise the bullying behavior of trucks. Most of us are at least mildly disturbed by the erratic habits of taxi drivers—except when we're in the back seat, of course. With the meter running we quietly applaud their performance. We're grateful—are we not?—that at least one other person understands the importance of our destination. Given these shifting allegiances, the notion of any objective right-of-way is as open to debate as where to find the best pizza or get the best coffee.

Evan Friss, in his book *On Bicycles: A 200-Year History of Cycling in New York City*, describes the enormous scale on which these negotiations play out each day. A professor and cyclist himself, Friss says that nearly "one quarter of the earth on which New York City sits is a street, roughly equal to fifty-eight Central Parks." Those streets, he argues, "reveal as much of the soul of the city as any place." He puts in concrete terms (if you'll pardon the expression) the vast terrain on which getting from point A to point B either intersects with, or bumps up against, the value system of other city dwellers. The question may be put as follows: If we sympathize with Allan Ripp's fears of getting splattered, yet we demand our takeout food post-haste; and if we curse the unruly behavior of taxi drivers, except when we're the ones behind the plexiglass, then what does that tell us about the nature of our soul?

It tells us that we're conflicted, of course.

I'm as guilty of this as anyone. Even as I try to peacefully coexist with my fellow New Yorkers, I still carry the selfish attitude of one person living among millions. I appreciate the complex tapestry that defines city planning, but I'm frustrated when that planning confounds my most immediate interests. I'm respectful of others who respect me back, but I'm more than willing to disregard those who've chosen to disregard me first.

My survival as a cyclist reflects what I was taught in driver's ed. Always anticipate the worst thing another driver might do, and be prepared to react. Defensive driving, in other words. Part of the bargain as a city cyclist is that I don't go very fast. Other riders pass me far more often than the reverse. Yet I'll admit to certain behaviors that test the limits, if not the letter, of the law. For example, there's the rolling stop at a quiet intersection; the blown-off traffic light when no one's around; or the "misdirection"—as I like to call it—down a one-way street. Imagine your destination lies just down the block, but the only way to get there is by making almost a complete lap around. It's hard not to shake your head in exasperation and steer your handlebars into oncoming traffic. That said, I'm mindful of going against the current, so I'll ride even slower and give a wide berth to oncoming cars. Oftentimes I'll wave in gratitude: a humble cyclist who doesn't think the road belongs to him. I'll even wave to police officers, who've surprised me on occasion by waving in return. Thus far (knock on wood), my only ticket has come from riding on the sidewalk. This was many years ago, during a crackdown after a cyclist badly injured an elderly woman in that same location. Even then, the policeman ticketed me for riding against traffic versus riding on the sidewalk, which he said would've incurred a much steeper penalty.

The first bicycle I ever owned was a navy-blue Schwinn: a starter bike with one speed and a white "S" printed on the seat. This was in the suburbs of Chicago; I might've been seven or eight years old. A few years later, I graduated to a black 10-speed (another Schwinn) with thin tires and handlebars that curled down like a pair of ram's horns. In those days, almost everyone owned a 10-speed. Sometimes you rode with your hands over the top crossbar, sometimes you palmed the hand brakes mounted on the sides. Sometimes, unbeknownst to your parents, you rode with no hands at all. No one gave it a second thought back then. On a quiet side street you sat back casually with your arms at your sides, or with your hands folded loosely in your lap. Whenever a car approached, you simply leaned forward and retook the steering again—no big deal. It was only while coasting down a steep hill, or if a friend challenged you to a race, that you would flatten your torso and drop your grip to the handlebars' lower curvature, like Greg LeMond in the Tour de France.

I was a rebellious kid in many ways. I mouthed off, took lots of stupid risks, and stuck my nose in plenty of places it didn't belong. But even at my most rambunctious, I would never have considered myself bold enough to ride a bicycle in New York City. All these years later, it's just the opposite. I have zero qualms about riding in New York, but I would sooner skateboard down a flight of stairs than steer my bicycle without hands.

When I moved here in 1998, cycling was more of a fringe activity: something reserved for riders in Central Park, for those daredevil messengers, and for deliverymen. The only cyclist I knew was a fellow grad student who wore his waist-length hair in a ponytail and sported spandex shorts around the department. A nice fellow, but widely regarded as an eccentric. New York was still in a rollerblading craze, and I quickly joined the movement. Living in Greenwich Village, I explored the city's downtown neighborhoods, visited my favorite cafés, rollerbladed to East River Park to play tennis or pickup soccer. The inconveniences were many. Rollerblades were seasonal, for starters. Secondly, few establishments allowed them indoors, so you had to bring extra shoes in a backpack and lug your blades around afterward. In the dog days of summer, the exertion from skating left you overheated and sweaty, especially when toting a laptop. Ultimately, rollerblades made great fun for recreational jaunts, but they were unsuited to everyday commuting.

From the early to mid-2000s, a steady rise in cycling began. The development and beautification of riverfront parks drew riders to miles and miles of scenic bike paths, while Mayor Michael Bloomberg saw two-wheeled commuters as part of a larger strategy to make the city greener. His campaign to create bike lanes and install bike racks by office buildings was amplified by the 2007 appointment of Janette Sadik-Khan to transportation commissioner. Her zeal for more bike lanes, and eventually protected bike lanes, led to citywide tensions with motorists, local politicians, and neighborhood leaders. The term "bikelash" made the cover of *New York* magazine, and resistance spanned from whiter, wealthier areas like Park Slope, Brooklyn, to more racially diverse and working-class neighborhoods like East Harlem. In the South Williamsburg section of Brooklyn, home to a sizable ultra-Orthodox Jewish community, the growth in bike lanes coincided with new condos and increasing gentrification. *New York* magazine's Michael Idov described it as the "Hasid-hipster standoff": a quarrel between longstanding community members who dressed in black and behaved conservatively, and an influx of riders who wore scantier outfits and conducted themselves far more immodestly.

Jeremiah Moss, who writes the *Vanishing New York* blog and published a book of the same title, insists that city initiatives like bike lanes "are not friendly to a diverse, affordable, and equitable urban environment." It's debatable, however, at least in New York, whether bike lanes create unwelcome changes to an area or simply respond to changes already under way. The scrutiny over such initiatives goes on. When New York's bike-sharing program began in 2013, residents decried the loss of street parking due to all the docking stations. Others fretted about the rise of congestion and increased danger from the armada of oversized, royal-blue bicycles, and the oblivious tourists who might use them. Such concerns have paled in comparison with the program's great success and wide acceptance. From 2013 to 2018, the fleet of Citi Bikes (so named for their corporate sponsor) doubled from 6,000 to 12,000, membership grew from 5,000 to 143,000, and the number of docking stations reached further and further into the outer boroughs.

Long before Citi Bike hit the streets, I purchased my first New York bicycle on Craigslist: a five-speed BMX with a white frame. At a bike shop I had plastic fenders attached so that I could ride in wet weather. A bike room in my building made for easy storage, and since theft was widely talked about, I dropped seventy-five dollars for a chain lock that made a fat coil around the seat post and doubled the bicycle's weight. I've gone through several more bikes since then. Some were stolen outright, others were knuckleheaded giveaways when I left them unlocked. The bike I owned the longest was a 1960s-era Raleigh Sprite cruiser. Picture the ugliest dirt-brown color, score the frame with missing paint, pock the fenders with scabs of rust, and you'll get the idea. I should mention, in full disclosure, that it was a ladies' bicycle. It's the type of bike that would've brought me endless torment and a few extra fistfights back in school. In New York City, a place where I'm too mindful of people's dress codes and their style of glasses, I'm not the least bit self-conscious about my bicycle. That includes the wire basket, which is one of my most essential possessions. The finicky derailleur I learned to put up with, just as I learned to get by with only five of ten working gears. But the loss of that basket would be almost as great a hardship as losing the bike itself.

To look at my junky old Raleigh, you'd consider it the farthest thing from a status symbol. But the bike carried a certain status nonetheless. I was reminded of this every so often, when a seemingly innocent encounter took on an unexpected friction. Such was the case during one Saturday afternoon bike ride in Brooklyn Heights. It was a pleasant summer day, I was riding down Court Street past the Cadman Plaza farmers market, and as I neared the intersection with Montague Street, the traffic light decided to turn red. I still had a good twenty feet to go, but that didn't stop the pedestrian in front of me from getting upset.

"You cyclists think you own the road!" she yelled.

The woman had good reason to be jumpy. She'd entered Court Street not by the clearly marked crosswalk, but on a diagonal line that put her right in my path.

I quickly drew to a stop. "The intersection's up there," I said, indicating behind her. Soon enough we were talking over each other, turning a deaf ear to the other's comments. A newly arrived pedestrian took up her cause, a man who hadn't even witnessed the event, but that made him no less vigorous in his anti-cycling crusade. I threw out a last, desperate jab—*Try using the crosswalk next time*—before I turned down Montague and escaped their twin flogging.

These entanglements have a cumulative effect. Divisions harden along party lines; righteous anger morphs into a pre-existing condition. Crowded streets provide easy kindling for such passions, and the flames, once ignited, become that much harder to put out. In my childhood I never saw cycling as anything more than a means of transportation, but in adulthood, like it or not, my bicycle has become an extension of who I am. In New York City, cycling fixes your identity in the same way as being a dog owner, belonging to the Park Slope Food Coop, or rooting for the Mets. Though I've never taken part in bicycle activism, I understand how cycling, all by itself, is interpreted by some as its own kind of statement. It's a form of expression that determines not only how others see you, but what sort of treatment you're liable to receive.

On a sunny September morning in my childhood home of Wilmette, Illinois, I found myself inside the Church of Jesus Christ of Latter-Day Saints. I'd always been curious about this weathered limestone building. Its lone steeple stands to the side like a watchtower; its curved front wing protrudes like a beached whale onto the front lawn. The visit to my parents coincided with Rosh Hashanah, and because their synagogue couldn't accommodate the High Holy Day surge, their temple had made arrangements with the Mormons across town.

Thankfully, the rabbi proceeded through the service at a good pace. As his sermon got under way, my mind drifted toward the corned beef and half-sour pickles waiting in my parents' fridge. Then the rabbi drew my attention again. He spoke about the tragic death of a young woman, just twenty-nine years old, who'd lost her life to a cement truck. The daughter of a congregation member, she'd been riding her bike in Williamsburg, Brooklyn, when the truck plowed into her at a major intersection. A terrible pall fell over the congregation. The rabbi said this was the sixteenth bicycle death in New York that year (it was actually the fifteenth), and from way back among the folding chairs, I trained my stare straight ahead and avoided eye contact with my parents. I particularly avoided looking at my mother, who had cut down on—but never quite relinquished—her warnings to her middle-age son. Every so often she would chide me for not wearing a helmet, and she would admonish me, above all, to *Be careful.*

The rabbi spoke about the preciousness of life. He mentioned God's command to Abraham—that he sacrifice his only son, Isaac—as a reminder of the difficult, often inscrutable, tests of our faith. Or at least that's what it sounded like. In truth, I was still rattled by the thought of that cement truck—and the poor young woman who'd been dragged through the street. The accident had occurred not four miles from where I lived. It struck me, as I sat beside my parents in the back of the Mormon church, that maybe cycling itself was an act of faith.

Aren't we constantly being reminded of our own vulnerability? News reports, social media, nervous relatives—even the streets we ride on keep us apprised. From time to time I'll spot a forlorn, seemingly abandoned bicycle chained to a street sign, its frame and tires painted entirely white, reminding me of an animal carcass with its flesh picked clean. These "ghost bikes," as they're called, honor crash victims with a small plaque attached to the handlebars. The original ghost bike appeared in St. Louis in 2003, and by 2005 the first one had shown up in New York. According to the Street Memorial Project, an advocacy group for cyclists and pedestrians, the citywide number reached 237 by the end of 2019, and the shrines had spread to more than 225 locations worldwide.

Even more than menacing drivers or inattentive cabbies, it is the parked car that frightens me most. To skirt past a long line of them, sleeping head to toe along the curb, is to ponder an unseen hand that at any moment might unleash a large flap of metal in your path. The door wings out perpendicularly—like a stop sign from a school bus—and leaves you but a split second to cut your speed or swerve around it. Thankfully, in all my years of riding, this has happened to me only once. The collision occurred on 12th Street in the West Village, as I was riding a Citi Bike to where I teach. An unusually steep line of cars backed up from the intersection with Sixth Avenue, and I was gliding past the unmoving vehicles when the taxi door presented itself—barely a bike length away. The distinct, unforgettable thought flashed through my mind: "Well, I guess this is happening."

What came next was more of a jumble. The physics of it, I mean. Somehow my torso folded over the door as the bicycle rammed into it. The bike fell sideways, my body slipped off the door, and—in the words of my skateboarding friend—I ate pavement. My legs split awkwardly over the fallen bicycle as my left hand bore the brunt of my weight. I noticed, from that semi-pushup position, that my messenger bag was slightly dislodged from the front rack, but I recall not thinking much of it at the time.

The man who emerged from the taxi offered an immediate apology. Before I had time to uncork my tirade, his show of concern put a stopper in it. He was a cyclist too, he told me. He always looked first before he opened a car door. "I'm so sorry I forgot—" he said shamefully.

I checked myself to make sure I was okay. My left hand was sore, but because I could rotate my wrist, I assumed nothing was broken. Then it occurred to me: Was I supposed to call the police? I asked the guy for his information. I told him I wasn't trying to be a jerk, and he graciously accommodated me. At the sidewalk I took out a pen and some scratch paper as he began dictating his name.

I stopped writing and looked at him. "Get *out* of here," I said. "You're kidding me."

How could I have possibly recognized him? My only picture of the guy dated back many years ago, when his hair had been much longer and he'd looked…well, let's just say a bit younger.

Not only had I read this man's work, but I'd used his short stories in one of my courses. He quickly turned bashful and thanked me. He mentioned his new novel that would soon be coming out, and he wondered if he could send me a copy. Once I'd jotted down his email we proceeded together along 12th Street, where we had a nice chat about teaching and writing. At Sixth Avenue we parted company, and in a few days I would email to let him know my hand was feeling much better. (I didn't bring up the cracked screen on my laptop.) Two weeks later, his book arrived at my apartment, and I began reading a humorous, racy novel with a surprising plot twist and a remarkably touching ending. Without giving away the story, or revealing the author's identity, I'll say only that the main character is a man trying to work through a lingering point of contention in his life—a man who will travel halfway around the world in an attempt to make things right—and by the end he discovers a spiritual side that might've been lurking within him all along.

So the rabbi talks of troubled faith. So the novelist writes of faith renewed. Who, then, will speak to the cyclist's troubled soul?

From time to time, in moments teetering on distress, the words of my anonymous rescuer float back to me. *Just let it go.* He offered this advice as he steered me away from an altercation I didn't have enough sense to abandon on my own. His face may be lost to me now, but I still take comfort, all these years later, simply by the thought of him. Just knowing such people walk among us brings a certain measure of relief. For all of us who travel on foot, get around by bicycle, or sit behind the wheel, it's extraordinary to imagine those rare individuals who always follow the rules of the road, even when they don't have to.

Hurricane Sandy: The Lights Go Down on Houston Street

THE YEAR BEFORE HURRICANE SANDY, the threat of natural disaster was already in the air. On an early August afternoon in 2011, I'd been in my kitchen preparing lunch when the dishes began to rattle inside the cabinets. Nothing unusual there. Whenever an oversized truck hit a pothole on Houston Street, the loud *whump* would send a mild shake through the building and stir the plates and saucers in the kitchen cupboard. On that particular afternoon, the clinking was a bit louder and lasted considerably longer. It occurred to me that it might've been my downstairs neighbors, who were having work done on their apartment—but hadn't they finished by now? The noise went on for a few more seconds until the plates gradually resettled, and the clattering faded away.

Ten minutes later, I'd already forgotten the incident when a special report came on TV. A 5.8 magnitude earthquake had struck Virginia, about a hundred miles from the nation's capital, and the tremors were felt as far north as Rhode Island. President Obama was on vacation, but the rest of the White House had been evacuated. In New York City, the quake occurred during an important press conference by Cyrus Vance, the Manhattan district attorney, who was announcing dropped charges against the head of the International Monetary Fund. Months earlier, the name Dominique Strauss-Kahn had splashed across the tabloids after he was hauled off an airplane in handcuffs at JFK, based on sexual assault accusations by his hotel chambermaid. Just as Vance's press conference got under way, his face swung between confusion and controlled astonishment. The floor started shaking, a sudden panic swept across the room, and reporters scrambled in all directions. Vance's handlers swooped in quickly to usher the district attorney offstage, and the press conference was promptly terminated.

Mother Nature wasn't done yet. Just a few days later, Hurricane Irene dominated the headlines as it nosed its way up the East Coast. Having lived through two hurricanes in Charleston, South Carolina, I was barely fazed by the news. That Saturday I attended a hurricane party in the West Village, where we drank, played board games, and watched episodes of *Mad Men* and *Curb Your Enthusiasm.* To call Irene the storm that never was would be inaccurate. New Jersey and Long Island suffered major damage, while upstate New York and Vermont were hit especially hard. But the city itself was mostly spared. In SoHo, some of the flooded streets reminded me of Venice, with dark channels of water lagooned between buildings. But the water was barely ankle-deep, and if you looked closely you could see the painted crosswalks just below the surface.

One year later, Sandy would more than make up for what her sister failed to deliver. In the fall of 2012, the country was already gripped by another brewing storm: the upcoming presidential election. Obama supporters were disheartened by how badly Mitt Romney had trounced the incumbent in the first debate. The former governor of Massachusetts and cofounder of Bain Capital had steamrolled Obama and seized control from the moderator like he was running his own board meeting. But Romney would give back ground a few days later, when a secret recording emerged of him at a fundraiser, where he called 47 percent of Americans "takers" who didn't pay taxes and expected handouts. It was a damning sound bite. The country was still digging out from the 2008 financial crisis—the worst recession since the Great Depression—and in Washington the opposition party cared more about kneecapping Obama than giving relief to suffering Americans. Mitch McConnell, the Senate minority leader, had stated from the outset that his top priority was to make Obama a one-term president. Going on four years later, a lot of us worried he might succeed.

At the end of October 2012, election fears fell into the background as hurricane fever washed over the city. The vibe inside pharmacies and grocery stories felt like being among squirrels in late autumn. Skittish customers lunged through the aisles as batteries and bottled water flew off the shelves. On Sunday, one day before Sandy's anticipated arrival, the MTA ended service early. Everything in the city seemed to be in the process of closing down, and by Monday afternoon the streets felt desolate. Still skeptical, I expected Sandy to have the same soft-gummed bite as Irene, although—it went without saying—I would attend my friend's hurricane party for the second year in a row.

A touch of rain moistened the late-afternoon air. A slightly amped-up wind shook the awnings as I walked through the West Village, searching for a café to read in before the party. The only open places were bars and bodegas, and at the Corner Bistro, on West 4th and Jane Street, I found a back table and had a plate of fries with a Coke ("We don't serve hot drinks," the waitress said). I strained to read amid the packed revelers and dim lighting, and by the time I'd eaten my last French fry, the situation outside had already changed. The wind lashed a lot harder, and a heavy, continuous rain soaked the streets. Under the last shades of dusk I walked to a nearby wine bar called Vin Sur Vingt, where the pre-party was taking place. Sandy continued to dial herself up by a few more notches. Some partygoers arrived with videos they'd shot at the Hudson River Park, and on a pair of phones I saw water slipping ominously over the sea wall. White-fringed wavelets skimmed the pedestrian pathway; they looked like shallow half-moons edging closer and closer to the lawn.

Over the loud music I couldn't hear the wind, but its strength was evident from the front windows. The lamplit trees were getting pummeled. The thin ones bent sideways as their leaves barely held on to the distressed branches. Every few minutes, another emergency vehicle streamed past on Seventh Avenue. I attempted several photographs of these, capturing only a slur of colors evaporating from view, until I finally snapped an intriguing shot of a fire truck in motion. It appeared as a swath of red, yellow, and white bands, looking more like the ghost of a fire truck than the real thing.

We were grateful for the short walk to my friend's apartment. The wind hounded us in the blustery dark, and we were forced to step around fallen branches that littered the street and crowded the sidewalk. Once inside, we forgot the elements and celebrated with more wine and mixed drinks. Sometime later, we were served a delicious stir-fry prepared by the host. Then Sandy came inside the apartment. The lights went dead—everybody *oohed* and *ahhed* with excitement—and in the candlelit apartment our socializing felt more decadent now that it was by candlelight. The mood didn't last. A few minutes later, a round of cell phone alerts went off: Con Ed reported an enormous piece of electrical equipment had been flooded, and it might take up to four days for the power to be restored. All at once, the party's momentum drained away. Some people chose to make their way home through the storm, others found friends in the neighborhood to crash with. A few of the guests, myself included, opted to wait out the storm at the party, which led to a miserable night on a shared futon with practically no sleep.

The next morning only a mild rain persisted, but the storm had a brutal tailwind. I dragged myself back through the deserted streets of the West Village, where store awnings snapped with relentless anger while overturned trash cans skidded about like playthings. All kinds of shrubbery blanketed the sidewalks—like the work of a maniacal leaf blower—burying fire hydrants and covering bicycles under thick canopies. Injured trees stood with arms dangling or broken off. Some trees had split cleanly from their trunks and lay as casualties on the pavement. One severed tree didn't make it that far. The riven treetop hung in the arms of its much larger neighbor, as if that neighbor didn't have the heart to let it go.

The power was out almost everywhere below 39th Street. After a bowl of cereal I slept for several hours, and with nothing to do in my cold, unlit apartment, I stuffed a camera, journal, and umbrella into my backpack and hopped on my bicycle. The rain had ebbed to a light drizzle that soon tapered off. On empty streets I saw leaves plastered to car windows, construction barricades knocked over, large traffic drums toppled or slanting precariously. Sometimes a harassing head wind would buck my handlebars dangerously off course or slow me down to a crawl. Other times, with the wind blowing from behind, I felt supercharged like something out of a slingshot.

My first stop was Tudor City Place. The genteel neighborhood sits on the eastern edge of Manhattan, just up the hill from Midtown, with an elevated view of the United Nations and a long span of the East River. On that day, the scenic background shrank beneath a flat, pewter sky. This pristine sliver of city had not been spared the ravages of Sandy. At the south end of a quaint, rectangular park, a large square of sidewalk had been thrust up by the powerful roots of two downed trees. Nearby, a black SUV sat with its windshield smashed into a spider's web of glass. An entire block of 43rd Street was closed off, as an enormous tree leaned with malicious intent against the front of a high-rise apartment. A team of firemen worked high up from a truck-mounted ladder, dismantling the tree with a buzz saw one slow branch at a time.

I continued north for a while. At East 70th and Lexington I stopped for two slices of Sicilian pizza before moving to a bakery across the street, where I drank coffee and wrote in my journal. By cell phone I reached a friend on the Upper West Side, who invited me to meet him for dinner, so I jumped back on my bicycle right as the rain resumed. My parents, had they seen me crossing Central Park via 86th Street, would've been justifiably appalled. I navigated the winding hill in the near dark, with one hand steering and the other holding up my umbrella like Mary Poppins. At the restaurant I drank a much-appreciated hot chocolate and, having already eaten, packed up most of the mac 'n' cheese I ordered. Afterward, my friend and I walked up Broadway under clearing skies before we parted company at 120th Street.

So began my long journey home. From Broadway I rode to West End Avenue and headed due south, which made for a scenic ride of splendid townhouses and regal apartments, one beautiful block after another, all the way down to 59th Street. Below 59th, West End changed to 11th Avenue and quickly lost its charm. In another twenty blocks or so, and a good twenty minutes after my journey had begun, I suddenly came upon a strange frontier. Behind me lay a glowing metropolis of lit windows and working street lamps, while ahead of me, for as far as I could see, the downtown buildings crouched in blackness. The entire island of Manhattan seemed divided in two. I was on the doorstep of an invisible city: a darkened patch of New York that had fallen off the grid and looked completely cut off from the rest of the world.

A giant explosion had taken place at the Con Ed substation on 14th Street, near the East River. The blast, which had zapped the power during my friend's party, was precipitated by a fourteen-foot tidal surge that inundated the transformer line while seventy-mile-per-hour winds battered the equipment. In one amateur video, you can see a small orange flame nipping at the side of the substation building, before the flame suddenly hatches into a giant white fireball. Two such blasts occurred, each within a few seconds of the other. The most striking footage comes in a video shot from Brooklyn, on the opposite side of the river, which reveals the true magnitude of both explosions. The two blasts obliterate the darkness and completely overwhelm the night sky, like a supernova overtaking the far reaches of outer space.

By Con Ed's assessment, some 1.4 million homes and businesses lost power within an area stretching from Staten Island to Pennsylvania. Many people evacuated lower Manhattan and stayed in hotels or with family and friends. The New York City Marathon was still on schedule for the following Sunday, but many hotels were now refusing to honor out-of-town reservations if it meant kicking out sheltering families. A friend invited me to stay at his aunt's large apartment on the Upper West Side, an option I might've considered if not for a lucky break in my neighborhood. NYU's student center remained open, thanks to a backup power source, and by teaching in their continuing ed program I was entitled to free meals in the cafeteria and access to its computer labs, lounges, Wi-Fi, and electrical outlets.

The late October sun departed well before dinnertime. At night I carried my detachable rear bike light and set it on blink, not to help guide me on the pitch-black streets but to make me more visible to other pedestrians and especially to cars. From a block away, the thin scrape of a flashlight beam would signal a fellow journeyman. Sometimes, if it were a group, a few thin strobes would mingle together. Several blocks ahead, the eyes of a disembodied vehicle would emerge out of the blackness, like a subway car from deep in its tunnel. Police officers in reflective jackets stood at major intersections, surrounded by a nest of pink flares, as they directed traffic. It was a reassuring sight to come upon in the dark, like a campfire to a traveler lost in the woods. At unmanned intersections, I waited my turn before aiming my blinking light at the halted traffic, acting as pedestrian and crossing guard at the same time.

There was no cell phone reception downtown, but people with landlines could still be reached. My trusty copper wires enabled me to keep in touch with my parents back in Chicago, and I also spoke with a friend on the Upper East Side, who invited me to Shabbat dinner and a clean shower. I was deeply moved by the offer, but by week's end I lacked the fortitude to make another commute uptown. I did manage to bathe myself, however. In nineteenth-century fashion, I heated two large pots of water on the gas stove, placed them on pot holders on the bathroom sink, and scrubbed myself with a wash cloth while standing in the bathtub. On the freezing porcelain I set down a small plastic basin and filled it with enough hot water to cover my toes and keep my feet warm. Washing was the easy part. Rinsing away the suds proved to be a tiresome and prolonged chore. In frustration I finally turned the pot upside down over my head, but even then I still had to duck under the icy tap water to get rid of the lingering shampoo.

More cold water was soon to follow. I'd brought home half sandwiches, bagels, and fruit from NYU's student center, which allowed me to avoid trekking there for each meal. As long as the refrigerator door was shut quickly, its interior kept relatively cool and things wouldn't spoil. One roommate of mine wouldn't grasp this concept. I was shocked to enter the kitchen one morning and find her staring inside the open fridge, her arms crossed as she pondered the shelves, like someone comparing channels on television. Against my reproach she simply shrugged and said, "What does it matter?—the fridge is going to get warm anyway."

There went my temper. The argument that ensued bore the same ugly complexion as all our previous fights, whose subjects ranged from unequal closet space to laundry left in the bathroom sink to other such banalities. I lacked the saintly tolerance of our third roommate, and these growing clashes meant an eventual reckoning would have to come.

I met a friend that night at La Lanterna on MacDougal Street. It was one of a handful of places that had obtained a generator and was open for business. An attractive Russian waitress, friendly yet skillfully immune to our flirting, took our orders. My friend drank wine while I took the waitress's suggestion and ordered a Hot Irish Nut: a lovely blend of decaf coffee, Bailey's Irish Cream, hazelnut liqueur, and whipped cream. For much of the night we talked politics. Mayor Bloomberg had rightly, if not belatedly, postponed Sunday's marathon. Even if hotel space weren't an issue, the race would've diverted police and other resources from more pressing needs. This was Friday, November 2nd, and with the presidential election a few days away, our feelings alternated between deep worry and deep resentment. For four straight years, the opposition had tried to beat back any legislation that might alleviate the financial crisis and shorten the enduring recession—all to avoid giving President Obama "a win." My friend and I took turns fuming until our drinks ran dry and we'd finally run out of adjectives.

That night—the fourth in a row—I brushed my teeth by candlelight and wore extra layers to bed. I fell asleep with the warmth of alcohol in my stomach, and warm thoughts of the waitress in my head. A few hours later I awoke to a mysterious sound. Something had gone bump in the night. One of my roommate's cats, I presumed—but as I sat up disoriented, I noticed a faint green light blinking from my nightstand. It was the LED of my clock radio. The power had returned, and I deduced that one of my electronic devices must have made some kind of clicking, or clunking, sound—triggered by its reanimated circuitry. I soon fell back asleep, but in another few hours I was awakened once more, this time by several sharp clangs of the radiator. The boiler was up and running again. It sent its steam throughout the building and began heating the water for my next morning's shower: the first real shower I would take in several days.

Some parts of the city still remained without power. Several subway stations remained closed from excessive flooding, while subway tunnels under the East River would require several months' repair from saltwater damage. One week after the storm, on the eve of the election, a New School colleague made a very astute remark. She said that all of us, no matter our political affiliation, would spend roughly half our lives under a president we didn't like. This was a sensitive and high-minded observation—and I was in no mood for it. How did one make peace with an opposition that lied about "death panels" in the Affordable Care Act, or who trafficked in falsehoods about the president being born in Kenya? How did one tolerate antiabortion zealots like the Senate candidate from Missouri, who claimed that a raped woman could never become pregnant, because in cases of "legitimate rape"—as he artfully described it—a woman's body would automatically shut down and not allow conception?

In that election, at least, America's better sense prevailed. The country chose Obama for a second term and rejected the two most radical candidates for senator. To celebrate I brought donuts to my Wednesday morning classes, and a few weeks later, while visiting my parents outside of Chicago, I ate a large share of turkey and watched a fair share of football. New Yorkers were in need of a pick-me-up, but the Jets refused to provide one. In their Thanksgiving game against the Patriots, they trailed 35-3 at halftime and committed one of the most embarrassing turnovers in football history. The quarterback, after botching his handoff to the running back, ran straight into the rear end of a three-hundred-pound lineman. He fell backward onto his own wallet, coughed up the ball to a defender for an easy touchdown, and created a highlight reel that quickly came to be known as "the butt fumble."

The city did find inspiration a few weeks later, at a December 12th benefit concert for Sandy relief. The lineup at Madison Square Garden included Bruce Springsteen, Alicia Keys, The Rolling Stones, Billy Joel, and many other A-list performers. The concert raised millions of dollars in aid while providing a moment of healing for the region. Unfortunately, the moment wouldn't last. Just two days later, in a small town some seventy-five miles north of New York City, a man entered an elementary school in Connecticut carrying a semiautomatic assault rifle, which he proceeded to fire upon trapped, terrorized, and defenseless children. When the shooting had ended, twenty young victims and six of their teachers lay dead.

Once more, the nation's collective sadness overflowed its banks. In a televised vigil from Newtown, Connecticut, home of Sandy Hook Elementary School, the newly reelected president said that Americans had some hard questions to answer. Was our country really doing enough to protect our children from danger? Were we really doing our best to make sure all our children lived out their lives to the fullest? A spiritual tone entered his voice. The president spoke of love's capacity to lead us through darkness, and he cited a passage from scripture that I'd never heard before, a decree from Jesus that said: "Let the little children come to me, and do not hinder them, for to such belongs the kingdom of heaven." A long pause followed. The president hung his head mournfully and began reading the names of every slain child. He read only the first names—like a teacher taking attendance—and by the third child I was already weeping. I imagined the tears of millions of Americans, all of us parked before our TV sets, but what I couldn't imagine—and what I didn't dare try to imagine—was the sorrow of all those parents who were forever robbed of these innocent young lives.

***

My roommate troubles reached their tipping point. The damage of so many skirmishes could no longer be smoothed over or buffed away: The entire flooring would have to come up. The person on the lease held all the power, so I was given my walking papers and a deadline. The friend who'd invited me to a shower and Shabbat dinner offered me some soothing words of advice, which helped chase away at least some of the bitterness. It was a Yiddish expression passed down from her grandmother—*Der klieger lut nuch*—which essentially meant: "The smarter one lets it pass." She reminded me that I was getting out of a bad situation—I should feel liberated. And as far as that roommate was concerned, my friend's grandmother had another wise saying: *Shpring in yam*. It was a wonderful little tidbit best translated as: "Go jump in the sea."

My friend was right, of course. But being freed of a difficult situation didn't make my apartment search any easier. The process inflicted the same aggravation and heartbreak as my previous searches, including a bait and switch so awful that I even consulted a lawyer. One skipped stone after another fell into the river, until a lucky stone finally made its way across. All the way across to Brooklyn, that is. On the other side of the East River, I landed in a neighborhood of beautiful side streets and historic charm: an area that resembled the Greenwich Village I'd adored for so long, and that I would soon fall for in the same way I'd fallen for downtown Manhattan all those years ago.

PART THREE

Brooklyn Envy

In the Heights

THE FIRST THING I EVER knew about Brooklyn was that it was the fourth largest city in America. I didn't understand how this was possible—Brooklyn wasn't even a city unto itself. But that's what a giant billboard proclaimed at the start of each episode of *Welcome Back Kotter*, as the show's theme music kicked off. The sitcom portrayed a ragtag bunch of academically challenged high school students, nicknamed the Sweathogs, who were taught by the earnest yet wisecracking Mr. Kotter. It wasn't exactly the slums, but these unpolished, un-ascendant characters—Italian, Black, Jewish, and Puerto Rican—all seemed destined to remain in the neighborhood. Next to the high-profile world of Manhattan, these were clearly people on the outside looking in.

Such was Brooklyn. Just take Ralph Kramden of *The Honeymooners*—the Bensonhurst bus driver who could barely furnish his apartment beyond an icebox and a kitchen table. Whatever scheme he cooked up to improve his life would inevitably backfire on him. Or take Tony Manero of *Saturday Night Fever*, the restless young man (played by the most famous Sweathog, John Travolta) who worked a dismal job in a hardware store, hung out with delinquent friends, and could only dream of dancing his way out of Bay Ridge. Then, of course, there was the comically pathetic childhood in Woody Allen's *Annie Hall.* The humiliating family arguments were as frequent and thunderous as the Coney Island roller coaster that rattled directly over their home.

Each of these stories delivered the same message: Brooklyn was a place you moved away from, not a destination.

By the time I arrived there in the winter of 2013, that sentiment had long since passed. In the early 2000s, the more industrial Williamsburg section had undergone a transformation similar to that of SoHo. Its affordable rents and proximity to Manhattan—just a short ride to Union Square by the L train—brought an influx of college students, artists, and converted lofts. This quickly raised the neighborhood's profile, and trendy cafés, bars, and restaurants soon followed, as did the higher rents and new construction. This movement would gradually spread throughout Brooklyn. It occurred neighborhood by neighborhood, from Carroll Gardens to Fort Greene; from Dumbo to Prospect Heights; from Gowanus to Bushwick. Even the more pristine places like Brooklyn Heights and Park Slope, with their reputations for old money or being overrun with baby carriages, saw their status elevated by the young professionals and outsiders they drew. In a reversal of fortune from the lost Brooklyn Dodgers, the borough poached its own sports franchise: the New Jersey Nets. The NBA team played in a billion-dollar arena that was christened with a concert by the mega-platinum rapper Jay-Z, a native son to Brooklyn, who derived his professional name from the J and Z subway lines of his childhood.

Brooklyn was hip. Brooklyn was beautiful. And Brooklyn rents were starting to approach those of Manhattan. The search for an apartment always turns out to be an education, but in

New York City it very often teaches the same lesson: Whatever you were hoping to find in a certain price range rarely ends up being available. Inevitably, you're forced to ask yourself hard questions about how much more you're willing to spend for a better location, how much extra for a decent bathroom, how much more for additional square footage. How much extra can you afford to squeeze out for all three?

I could only squeeze myself so much further. On Houston Street I'd been paying $780 a month in a rent-stabilized apartment share, and just about every studio I saw was double that amount. So I ended up splitting the difference. I dropped from two roommates to one, bumped my rent up to $1,200, and took the smaller of two bedrooms on the top floor of a Brooklyn Heights townhouse. I'd often joked that my place on Houston Street was a pre-war apartment, with the punchline that it was pre–Gulf War. My new home on Hicks Street actually predated the Civil War. Built in 1848, the red-brick townhouse belonged to a single family that occupied the first and second levels. The grandmother lived on the third floor, and the entire fourth floor was rented to a man in his late thirties who worked in nonprofit. He interviewed me once, read a few references, and accepted me.

I was over the moon. The guy struck me as laid-back, perhaps a bit aloof, though his partner, a schoolteacher who lived in another state, was very friendly. I saw their pairing as a good sign. In the rear of the apartment, my bedroom was the size of a study, with a slanted ceiling that I would forgetfully knock my head against from time to time, and a postage-stamp window that overlooked the adjoining backyards of multiple townhouses. The living room was the apartment's crown jewel. From the fourth-floor landing, the front door opened to an old hardwood floor of an expansive parlor, whose opposite wall was inlaid with bookshelves from end to end, and whose centerpiece was a nonworking fireplace painted eggshell-white and framed by a decorative wooden mantle.

I was teaching a course that semester called Jews in America, and in its honor I booked Moishe's Movers to bear me across the river. On a Wednesday morning, three men swooped into my Houston apartment with the efficiency of a pit crew at the Indianapolis 500. They packed up the truck, drove out to Brooklyn, and walked everything up three flights in what must've been record time. There was one thing I couldn't bring with me to my new apartment: my home phone number. This marked the end of my 2-1-2 area code, and without a phone jack I couldn't even replace it with the trendy 7-1-8 call sign of Brooklyn. I had only the amorphous 9-1-7 area code to my name—a vague identifier for cell phones that spanned all five boroughs.

A friend and historian liked to remind me that Brooklyn Heights was the city's first suburb. (In spite of the sign from *Welcome Back Kotter*, the borough had consolidated with New York in 1898.) I'd often thought of this neighborhood as elegant but stodgy—sort of like Brooklyn's version of the Upper East Side—with its multi-million-dollar mansions on Columbia Heights and its pipeline to Wall Street. It was a shortsighted view that overlooked the neighborhood's more subtle flavor (just as it did with the Upper East Side, to be fair). Not simply an encampment for families, nannies, and strollers, the area contained a mix of professionals, graduate students from Brooklyn Law School, and undergraduates from various colleges who dormed in the old St. George Hotel. The neighborhood had its share of quality pubs, dive bars, and cafés—although, consistent with city trends, many would struggle with the ever-increasing demands of their landlords.

In 2013, on the north side of Brooklyn Heights, you could find the Henry Street Ale House, a wine bar, a café called Vine-apple, a Gristedes grocery store, and several restaurants of various ethnicities, plus a local, cash-only favorite called Noodle Pudding. There was a video rental store—one of the city's last remaining—and the Brooklyn Heights Cinema: an art house theater with two screens. Years before, I'd gone there to see *No Country for Old Men*, by the Coen Brothers, and shortly after my move I went to see *Silver Linings Playbook*, which would be nominated that year for Best Picture. Sadly, both the video store and the movie theater would close within the next two years.

In downtown Brooklyn Heights, about a ten-minute walk south of the St. George Hotel, Montague Street offered the cozy atmosphere of a small-town Main Street. The four-block stretch included clothing stores, a frame shop, hardware store, multiple cafés and restaurants, a chain grocery store, plus a couple of smaller, fancier supermarkets. One of these—I was thrilled to discover—carried the Pugliese bread I had long adored from Sullivan Street Bakery, the old store I used to frequent in SoHo. Gone, by then, was Heights Books, a fantastic used bookstore where I'd once brought my Texas friend from Miami of Ohio, who found his short story collection on the shelf and signed it for the owner.

On the southern edge of Brooklyn Heights, where Atlantic Avenue divided the neighborhood from Cobble Hill, stood a treasured emporium called Sahadi's. It was Brooklyn's equivalent of Zabar's, the legendary market on the Upper West Side. Sahadi's sold smoked fish, all kinds of cheeses, Middle Eastern and Greek dishes, an assortment of olives, various roasts of coffee, and what one colleague at The New School called the best hummus in the city. There were several dive bars along Atlantic, an upscale bar with an indoor bocce ball court, and an English pub called the Chip Shop. At the Roebling Inn—named after Washington Roebling, the former Union Army officer and Brooklyn Bridge engineer—you could drink craft beers, play Skee-Ball, and see a photo of the great Sandy Koufax every time you used the bathroom.

In my wanderings through Brooklyn Heights, I was constantly reminded of the West Village. Instead of the Hudson River on its western border, the East River would present itself in inviting glimpses from a couple blocks away. For every quaint side street like Barrow, Charles, or Perry, Brooklyn Heights had a Willow Street, Cranberry Street, or Garden Place. Here was a neighborhood of lovely townhouses, brownstone churches, clapboard homes with wooden shutters, converted carriage houses, grandiose mansions in Victorian or Renaissance styles, and glamorous high-rises with magnificent façades. Here and there, an occasional modern building muscled its way in, showing a brute indifference to its neighbors. Such incursions had prompted the area's landmarking efforts of the 1960s, when surveyors undertook the painstaking task of going block by block, lot by lot, to describe in precise detail the architectural features of each property. In this way, Brooklyn Heights became the city's first designated historic district.

Just beyond Atlantic Avenue, as I followed Henry Street into Cobble Hill, an impressive red-brick edifice appeared on my right. It was decorated with ornate stone details in a neoclassical design. The central wing was set back from the street, while its two protruding wings formed an H-shaped courtyard with a gated playground. This was Long Island College

Hospital. It was where my father, as a medical student at SUNY Downstate, had done rotations in obstetrics and internal medicine. Not long after I moved to the neighborhood, the hospital would meet the same fate as the Brooklyn Heights Cinema. Purchased by developers, the grand old building would be converted into high-priced luxury apartments, although an emergency-care facility, operated by NYU, would remain at the far end of Amity Street.

That winter marked the hundredth anniversary of Grand Central Station. (Its true name was Grand Central Terminal, but no one called it that.) It also marked the passing of Ed Koch, the colorful, rambunctious former mayor who'd taken helm of the city during its blight and financial turmoil of the late seventies, and who'd helped oversee the start of its recovery. I was teaching two courses that winter: my Jews in America class at The New School, and an eight-week continuing ed class on American short fiction, at NYU. I was still freelance copyediting at magazines one week per month, and I'd begun writing book reviews for *Time Out New York*. Over the years, I had published a number of short stories, reviews, and essays, but my first novel, after a long slog and multiple revisions, had hit the skids. I'd found a home for it with a small press that at first seemed like a great fit, before the press's ongoing dysfunction gradually drained away my enthusiasm. Long periods of silence were followed by promised edits that never arrived, until my level of distress reached a point that I finally pulled the plug.

Thus was I feeling very self-helpy around that time. I came across a line by Joyce Carol Oates, from a source I can no longer place, in which she proclaimed that "The novel is the affliction for which only the novel is the cure." What a stunning insight that was. Anyone who's ever labored on a novel will immediately identify with it. I took it to mean that going back to work was the only antidote for when the work seemed to be failing. And yet I wasn't sure how this applied specifically to me. Did it mean going back to take one more stab at revising that first novel, or should I keep my nose pointed forward and fight through the next one?

I kept in mind the words of another writer, Philip Levine, from a talk he'd given several years earlier. Reflecting on his own long journey, the poet had said that he didn't really discover his own voice until he was in his forties. To his audience of grad students at NYU, Phil—as he was affectionately called by everyone—was considered a tough but beloved workshop leader. He was a Midwesterner who populated his poems with working-class types like himself, and who still gave the impression—in spite of his distinguished career—of being a blue-collar writer. Rake-thin and bespectacled, he owned a gruff voice and a fiendish, sometimes withering, sarcasm, so later that evening, when he pulled up next to me in the bathroom, I couldn't resist saying hello. It was just the two of us, and from my neighboring urinal I nodded to him with a quick glance and said: "Wow, you really are human, after all." The esteemed poet laughed heartily, and without missing a beat, he made me promise him I would never tell another soul.

It was a season of double weather reports. The radio would announce the temperature as 28 degrees, only to add that the windchill felt like 15. This was no hiccup of cold air; it was a long, sustained throat clearing. Over several days we didn't get above freezing. I wore thermal underwear plus the trio of hat, scarf, and gloves, but on a tiny strip of exposed forehead I still felt a small visor of pain, like an ice cream burn on the roof of your mouth. In early February, a light snowfall blanketed the streets and made a wonderland of the city. From my bedroom window I saw the backyard decks, slatted tables, and garden planters brought together by a soft skin of snow. It was only a warm-up for more intense snowfalls to come. Great gobs drifted down on plumb lines, adhering to everything they touched along the way. No tree limb, no matter how crooked or misshapen, could escape its reach. On the streets, all the trash cans, front stoops, and parked cars succumbed to a unifying balm of white. The air looked sugarcoated. The snow would sanitize the roads and sidewalks for a few hours, until the effects were slowly eroded by grime and slush. Sometimes the snow was in no mood to stick around. The flurries resembled a mad swarm of bees returning to the hive, with each flake disappearing just as soon as it touched pavement.

It soon became the winter of my discontent. There was something peculiar about my roommate's behavior. Beneath his quiet demeanor lay an aggressive silence, which kept us from settling into any kind of normal conversation. Whenever I spoke to him, he would suddenly turn twitchy and seem impatient, as if I'd interrupted him or he were in between things. This laid-back manner, I also discovered, was really a form of carelessness: a front for someone who couldn't be bothered. It explained why there was no shower liner in the bathroom, just a terry-cloth curtain, and no drain board underneath the washed dishes. I bought these both without a word of thanks—without even the slightest acknowledgment. Nor did he acknowledge when I vacuumed up his blue corn chips from the living room rug or scrubbed his dried mouthwash off the sink. The one time he did address me was when I used the frozen gel pack in the freezer for my sore arm. "Could you ask me first next time?" he said. And then, before I could answer, he changed his mind and said, "Could you just not use it?"

I had been there two and a half months. I was grateful for the start of April, which rolled back the Canadian air and padded each afternoon with a little more daylight. It took me out of the apartment more and allowed me to venture farther out into surrounding neighborhoods. Springtime in Brooklyn Heights meant fertile blossoms on the trees, kids zipping around on Razor scooters, and church goers dressing up in more colorful garb. There was a new bounce in everyone's step, and for my birthday I asked my roommate's permission to throw a small party in the apartment. Naturally, I invited both him and his partner. The partner remained as energetic and outgoing as ever, and I often wondered at the contrast in their personalities. During weekend visits, the partner would initiate conversation and trade stories with me about teaching. His keen interest in the party was as evident as my roommate's disdain for it. In spite of granting his approval, he was clearly upset about the event. My *asking* was what upset him, I had the feeling. I had darkened the water with a few more drops of tension, but I decided not to lose sleep over it. Hadn't I scrubbed the toilet and run the vacuum cleaner enough times to earn the right? More than enough times, I firmly believed.

I made the rounds of the local establishments: Fresh Start Marketplace, Lassen and Hennings, Sahadi's, Key Food. At Montague Wine and Spirits, while signing my credit card slip, I did a double take of an old man browsing in back. Were my eyes deceiving me? I plucked my receipt and moved as swiftly as felt safe in a room full of racked bottles. It was him alright. I introduced myself as a former student in NYU's creative writing program, and Phil Levine could not have been more gracious. He welcomed me to the neighborhood that he himself was very fond of, and when I mentioned my fourth-floor walk-up on Hicks Street, he spoke wistfully about the charm of taking stairs in an old building.

I had a lot more to say, but I didn't want to push his kindness. So I didn't ask him if he remembered our bathroom encounter from years ago. Nor did I thank him for reading my favorite poem of his at two different events, each time at my specific request. That poem was called "A Theory of Prosody." It was a short, tender piece that paid tribute to a cat named Nellie, who had waited in the poet's chair each morning and would swipe at his hand whenever the line he wrote went on too long. Years later, the memory of Nellie's paw was a reminder to him, as much as any other lesson, about the great value in literary restraint.

The landscape changed again in May. You couldn't walk more than a few blocks without seeing the same piece of new-fangled architecture along the curb: a row of waist-high plasticky gray slits, roughly a foot apart, some twenty or thirty of them joined at the bottom by a strip of similar gray plastic. They looked like a line of coin slots as tall as fire hydrants, only with no conceivable purpose. In fact, these were the first docking stations for the city's bike-sharing program. Before long, a small armada of identical two-wheelers would inhabit these docks. The frames were bulkier than normal-size, the color an eye-popping blue, and the tires ruggedly obese. To top it off, these ugly machines were branded in several places with the corporate CITIBIKE logo.

My teaching brought me back to Manhattan a couple times per week, as did seeing my friends on occasional evenings or weekends. I was sad to discover that Joe's Dairy had closed. The tiny store on MacDougal Street had sold the city's best mozzarella (*MOOT-zeh-rella*, as my longtime Village friend pronounced it). It came as a fresh warm lump wrapped in tissue paper that they packed inside a brown paper bag. Luckily, Raffetto's on Houston Street was still going strong, as the family-run grocery store owned its property and was protected from escalating rents. On another trip to the Village, I attended the retirement party for the director of NYU's Expository Writing Program. He was the man I'd met a decade and a half earlier, in Charleston, South Carolina, without which I might never have come to New York in the first place.

Just as I was entering my third season in Brooklyn Heights, I learned that I would have to start hunting all over again. My roommate informed me that his partner would be moving in at the end of June, and I needed to be out by then. That was less than a month away. Could I have just a little bit longer, I asked him, if I ended up needing another week or two? He shook his head and said, "That's not possible." He stated this as if the decision were out of his control. I reminded him of our interview, in which he'd said he specifically wanted someone who'd stay at least a year, not to mention the hundreds of dollars I'd just spent on my move. "Things happen," he said with a shrug—and that's what finally set me off. Here was that careless detachment again. Here was that mild manner which really disguised a deeper selfishness. I won't pretend I took it well. For several minutes I dressed him down as he sat on the sofa, where he remained mute and firmly unapologetic. He deflected my rising anger with a stoic, almost impressive, indifference—until I finally accepted that the guy wasn't going to budge. From that moment on, we carried out all communication by email.

Smartphones had been around a few years, but I'd been one of the holdouts. I saw the way they owned people's attention as they walked down the street, and I feared turning into that exact person. Now the choice was no longer mine. I needed a smartphone to check apartment listings and email on the go, so I purchased an LG from the RadioShack on Court Street. The rental market hadn't softened a bit in the past six months, and I very quickly widened my search to include Prospect Heights and Bedford-Stuyvesant. I weighed the marginal savings in these more distant neighborhoods against the longer commute to my teaching and freelancing. One night, while I was watching a PBS documentary called "Nature's Deadliest Predators," I learned the term "envenomated" from the narrator. It described what happened to prey under the influence of an animal's toxin, and I couldn't think of a better word for my own situation. Each day, after another round of apartment hunting, I would try to keep my thoughts from becoming envenomated. Just the sound of my roommate's footsteps could do it, let alone what happened whenever our paths crossed.

The days ticked by. The end of the month drew closer and closer, and my anxieties continued to mount. On the StreetEasy website I kept getting lured in by the same listing: a Brooklyn Heights studio that was surprisingly under market rate. There was a good reason for it. The garden-level apartment was not only on the small side, but its size was further reduced by a three-step landing that protruded into the sunken living room (think *Three's Company* or *Mister Rogers' Neighborhood*). Add to that a wooden loft from the previous tenant, no closets, and a hideous linoleum floor, and it made sense that this unit had stuck around. And yet the studio, when I finally saw it in person, turned out to be far more appealing. It featured extra-high ceilings, giant double windows at the front and back, and a separate kitchen area in the rear. The tall coffered ceiling made the studio feel more spacious, while the plentiful light made it a lot more welcoming.

I decided to take it. I emptied my bank account, borrowed money from my parents, and ponied up the first, last, and second-to-last months' rent, plus a security deposit and a hefty broker's fee. The rent was $1,595. At my request, the landlord disassembled the loft, which left four dark squares in place of the missing posts. He also put in a white particle-board wardrobe that he propped up on thin wooden blocks to stand it level. ("Everything in Brooklyn is crooked," he said, in reference to the slanted floor.) Moishe's was booked through July, but I lucked into a small moving company that I happened to pass on the street while they were out doing a job. The young men were as strong as football players and about as inexperienced, so on moving day I ended up bringing down several boxes and helping them load up the sprinter van. On June 21st, the beginning of summer, I slept at my new place for the first time. I awoke early—to a flood of light from the kitchen windows—which looked upon an empty cement courtyard. In the afternoon, the street-facing windows poured sunshine into the living area. One by one, I acquired a used loveseat from Craigslist, an Ikea table and chairs, plus a coffee table and wooden armchair from an apartment sale. In the coming weeks, I arranged my bookshelves, set down multiple area rugs, and began hanging up photographs until the place gradually started to feel like my own.

How to describe the one-block street I'd landed on? Columbia Place was an oddity. It was the least known street to me in all of Brooklyn Heights. Only a short walk to Brooklyn

Bridge Park and the waterfront, the secluded lane sat between State Street and Joralemon (pronounced *Jur-OWL-uh-min*). The architecture could not be more eclectic. On one side of the street stood a row of clapboard houses with front porches, a few unappealing gray brick buildings (my own included), a small nursery school, and a handful of traditional red-brick townhouses. Across the street was a ruddy red-brick colossus, six stories high, that took up more than half the block. Its handsome façade consisted of wrought-iron railings and a series of arched galleries on each level (intended, way back when, to aerate the building and prevent the spread of disease). Originally constructed for laborers and dockworkers, it now housed overpriced units above a couple of boutique restaurants, a high-end bodega, a veterinarian's office, and the small laundromat where I would do my clothes.

The one-way road banked left as it turned into State Street. To the right of this rounded, two-way intersection was a narrow strip of community garden that backed against the concrete wall of the Brooklyn-Queens Expressway. Beyond the intersection lay a small, gated park that was mostly blacktop and largely unremarkable. It offered a few pieces of playground equipment, a tiny fitness area, some basketball nets, and little scenic value beyond a scattering of trees around its perimeter. For a long time, I walked right past this place and barely gave it a second thought, but a day would come when this park with a strange name and a tiny footprint would take on a surprising significance: not just for me personally, but for the larger neighborhood, the city itself, and the troubled times that would sweep across our country.

The Vandals of Adam Yauch Park

ADAM YAUCH PARK IS LESS a park than a medium-size playground in search of a school. From end to end it's a block long, an irregular lane squeezed between a parking garage and the on-ramp for the Brooklyn-Queens Expressway (BQE, in local speak). A bird's-eye view reveals an unlikely streak of blacktop: a skid-mark smudge of pavement that resembles an "S" shape. One entrance lies at the bottom of State Street, where it dead-ends with Columbia Place; the other entrance sits beside Atlantic Avenue, on a spur of sidewalk that briefly skirts the BQE on-ramp until the fence gate cuts it off. Most people never make it that far. Instead, they continue down Atlantic as it dips under the expressway and carries on toward the river. Blink—or keep your eyes on merging traffic—and you'll miss that entrance entirely.

This isn't a park you go to for the scenery. In this jagged corner of Brooklyn Heights, you won't find manicured gardens, well-groomed lawns, or handsome views of surrounding townhouses. The park's most prominent feature is an enormous jungle gym with red support beams and mustard-yellow railings, which provide a wash of color in this otherwise paved terrain. Behind the jungle gym sits a smaller climbing unit: a two-car locomotive with a barreled snout and a black stovepipe mounted on top. In November of 2016, just a few days after the presidential election, a rash of graffiti turned up on the locomotive's side panel. The black spray paint alarmed parkgoers, sent shockwaves through the neighborhood, and rippled all the way to the evening news. Two crude swastikas floated above a scrawl of letters that read: "Go Trump." It was a message delivered in celebration, in warning, or perhaps both.

When I first encountered the park, shortly after moving to Columbia Place, I had no idea who Adam Yauch was. I mistakenly pronounced the last name *Yow-CH*, not *Yow-K*. It seemed an odd choice for an odd piece of property. But Adam Yauch, I soon learned, was a big deal. He'd been a member of the Beastie Boys: a trio of Jewish rap musicians from Brooklyn who were popular in the 1980s and '90s. Of course I'd heard of the group, but all these years later I couldn't name any of their hits. An adoring fan quickly reminded me: "(You Gotta) Fight for Your Right (to Party!)," "No Sleep Till Brooklyn," and "So What'cha Want." The first song I recalled as a juvenile clamor of rebellion; the second I had (shamefully) never listened to before; but the third I seemed to remember more fondly. A visit to YouTube confirmed this. The song had a thumping drumbeat and a deep bass undercurrent: a rawness of sound combined with an explosive punk energy. I was instantly hooked. Here was a music that—like the jumping, gesticulating young men in the video—refused to be held back. I added the song to my "Rap" playlist on Spotify, a move that substantially diversified my limited repertoire.

Michael Diamond, Adam Horovitz, and Adam Yauch. Their respective stage names were "Mike D," "Ad-Rock," and "MCA." In the video of "So What'cha Want," the trio sport baggy jeans with rolled-up cuffs, wool ski caps pulled down to their eyebrows, and either tight T-shirts or—in the case of Yauch—an ugly plaid button-down in brown, white, and gray. Long before today's hipsters descended on Williamsburg, Bushwick, or Gowanus, the hipster attire already seemed prefigured by the Beastie Boys. As a child, Yauch lived in Brooklyn Heights at a time when the city struggled with bankruptcy, people were fleeing in droves to the suburbs, and this particular area was not as upscale as it's become (the exception, of course, being artists and writers). The group's identity might've been Jewish, but Yauch himself seemed more complicated. He was the son of a mixed Catholic-Jewish marriage, and later he became a practicing Buddhist. He trekked across Nepal, organized concerts in support of Tibetan freedom, and even met the Dalai Lama. Tragically, Yauch was diagnosed with cancer of the parotid salivary gland in 2009, for which he underwent treatment and surgery over the next few years. At the time, the Beastie Boys were at work on another album (they'd already sold forty million). In April of 2012, the trio would be inducted into the Rock & Roll Hall of Fame, but Yauch's condition kept him from attending. The following month, at the age of forty-seven, he passed away.

Most people only view this park as a byway between State Street and Atlantic. They hurry through this shortcut with the same disinterest as express-train riders speeding past a local station. And why wouldn't they? The playground offers but a scattering of trees and an elevated border of plantings and shrubs that barely conceal the massive concrete wall of the BQE on-ramp.

In summertime, flowering bushes and occasional daffodils help fill out this border, but even then the greenery still feels peripheral to the park—more like a sideshow than the main event.

To come upon it for the first time, you might believe this playground had been plopped down by accident or inserted to fill some preexisting void. Either impression would be fairly accurate. The park's founding dates back to Robert Moses, when the land was acquired as part of his plan to build the Brooklyn-Queens Expressway. The park opened in 1947 as the Atlantic Playground. The site was a tiny offshoot of leftover property (.395 acres, to be exact) abutting the BQE. Over the years, it would change names three more times: to State Street Park, Palmetto Playground, and—in May of 2013—to Adam Yauch Park. The former Beastie Boy had played on this lot as a child, and to mark the one-year anniversary of his passing, Palmetto Playground was rededicated in his honor. One month later, I would move into a small studio on Columbia Place, and for a long time I traversed this playground with no clue about its significance—and certainly no idea about how consequential it would become.

During the summer, the population in the park swells. The jungle gyms teem with children; kids crowd the narrow thruway waving giant bubble wands or tossing a football. A father and son play H-O-R-S-E on the half basketball court, next to which a young man rattles off pull-ups in the small fitness area. A steady stream of foot traffic shuttles between State and Atlantic, constantly rerouting a small pack of skateboarders. Every day, it seems, another birthday party gets thrown at the two stone picnic tables by State Street. Just a short distance away, a metal spigot rises waist-high from the cement to shoot up an umbrella of water. Kids dart in and out of the showery circle, some sticking their body parts directly in the spray, some craning their heads back to receive a drink. Parents keep watch from a nearby cluster of benches, and they're not alone. A pair of cast-iron bears (not quite life-size) stand guard with their heads alertly turned, their front paws in the pose of a dog on its hind legs.

Tucked behind the parking garage, and nearly invisible to most of the playground, sits a full-length basketball court surrounded by a chain-link fence. Blacks, whites, Asians, and Indians compete here in spirited bouts of five-on-five. It's impossible to walk by without hearing some version of trash talk or witnessing play get halted to debate a foul. Amazingly, both the full court and the neighboring half court get used year-round, at all hours of the day, and in all weather. One night, on my way back from the grocery store, I came upon three teenagers shooting lazily at the half court's metal backboard. "You know it's raining, right?" I asked sarcastically while walking past. They laughed good-naturedly, shrugged at one another, and resumed playing.

Another group that frequents the park in summer are Jews. I don't mean Jews like myself, who dress the same as the other neighborhood residents. I'm talking about Orthodox Jewish families who commute from more distant Brooklyn neighborhoods like Midwood or Crown Heights. They dress in self-identifying clothing: The father wears black trousers and black vest, a white button-down, hanging tzitzit on the hips, a black yarmulke, and side curls of hair over each ear. The young boys wear the same yarmulkes and side curls, though in place of their father's black-and-white ensemble they have on long pants and identical striped long-sleeve shirts. The girls wear conservative-patterned dresses or plain blouses with long skirts and dark stockings. The siblings often match clothing by gender, if they're close in age, and their outfits quickly distinguish them from the other kids on the playground. The mothers, if they happen to come along, wear similar plain blouses and long skirts, dark stockings, and a head covering of a scarf or headband.

Sunday is the day the Orthodox come most often (Saturday being the Sabbath). They arrive at the park in an orderly fashion: a family that stays in close orbit of the father. Once inside, however, a shift occurs. All reserve falls away as the children make haste for the jungle gyms, where they scoot across the planked bridges or attempt to climb the twisting spine of monkey rings, which look like an upside-down centipede. At the drinking fountain, the brothers behave in the familiar, devilish attitude of young boys. They needle one another as they fill water balloons, sometimes harassing their little sister. Left alone, the girl skips about or shuffles her feet in a private little dance, as young girls often do. Their behavior is a welcome and joyful surprise to me. Seeing these kids run around like any other children on the playground makes me realize that I'm the only one here who feels awkward, the only person burdened by his insecurities.

Was it Yauch's celebrity in a successful, mainstream Jewish group—or was it the visible presence of these Jews—that elicited the odious spray paint back in November of 2016? Two days after its discovery, an anti-hate rally was held in the park. Supporters filled the open playground and wedged together among the lookout nooks and bridges of the jungle gym. Beastie Boy Adam Horovitz ("Ad-Rock") addressed the crowd by megaphone, speaking through the handheld attachment mic like a CB radio. He summed up the vandalism in simple terms, boiling it down to "someone in New York City linking Nazi Germany to Donald Trump in a 'hell yeah' kind of way. In a park—" he reminded everyone, "—where children play."

His voice had the inflected tone of a politician's. He rattled off a list of other incidents around the country—toward Jews, Blacks, and Muslims—until, with growing anger, he described the episode of a "white guy at a Starbucks in Florida who called a woman of color 'trash' and 'garbage' because she didn't produce his latte in time." As his voice grew louder, traces of his Brooklyn accent came out more clearly. According to Horovitz, this Florida man claimed *he* was the one who'd been discriminated against—as a white guy, as a Trump supporter—and Horovitz, shaking his head in disbelief, could only add: "*Come* on!" As in: "*Get* real." It sounded like a lyric from one of their rap songs. Gray-haired and approaching fifty, Horovitz owned the same chutzpah as the brash young singer he used to be. Like the rest of his bandmates, he was not afraid to call it like he saw it.

In 2016, I had hoped this might be a passing phase. I had wanted to believe the perpetrators, satisfied with acting out, would return underground or recede back into the dark corners of the internet. A naïve belief, as it turned out. I was not—as Yauch himself once sang—"wise to the demise." In the years since his playground was defaced, a spike in harassment and hate crimes had been tracked by the Southern Poverty Law Center, the Anti-Defamation League, and several other organizations. To its historical record, America added the Unite the Right rally in Charlottesville *("Jews will not replace us")*, the mass shooting at the Tree of Life Synagogue in Pittsburgh, the stabbing to death by sword of a Black man in Times Square, and—on the second to last night of Hanukkah, at the end of 2019—a machete-wielding assailant at a Hasidic rabbi's home in Monsey, New York. Governor Andrew Cuomo was quick to label this an act of domestic terrorism, adding that "If anyone thinks that something poisonous is not going on in this country, then they're in denial, frankly."

In downtown Brooklyn, a *No Hate. No Fear.* demonstration took place eight days after the Monsey stabbings. It was the first Sunday of 2020, a bright but cold afternoon with a blustery wind that snapped the high-strung flags of Cadman Plaza. In some ways my attendance felt like a half gesture, as I hadn't joined the supporters—some ten thousand strong—who'd marched from lower Manhattan across the Brooklyn Bridge. Instead, I met up with them afterward in the Columbus Park section of the plaza. A row of giant tourist buses, having trucked in demonstrators from several states, lined the park. The police presence was profoundly visible. Officers patrolled the park on foot; they stood guard at closely spaced intervals around the plaza; and they manned the abundant squad cars, SUVs, and "Disorder Control" vans on the otherwise closed-off streets. Their numbers were staggering to look at, while the vehicles they came in might've equaled the entire fleet of a small city.

I wasn't the only late arrival. Other demonstrators kept filing into Columbus Park, taking up space on the artificial soccer field and tiled pathways. A raised platform stood in front of the massive granite wall of the Brooklyn War Memorial, flanked by the memorial's two giant statues. One of these symbolized "victory," the other "family." A leader from the United Jewish Appeal (UJA) Federation stirred the crowd by saying: "Any attack against a visibly Orthodox Jew is an attack against all

Jews, all New Yorkers, and all people of goodwill." That brought loud cheering and a wave of applause. From one of the large viewing screens, I watched Devorah Halberstam, a longtime activist and the mother of a Hasidic teenager murdered on the Brooklyn Bridge back in 1994. She offered her listeners a stern warning: Jews were the "canaries in the coal mine," she told us. They were always the first targets of attack whenever the forces of hate began to unleash themselves. Her voice was both husky and high-pitched. Sometimes she sounded anguished, other times angry. Because of how close she stood to the microphone, her words were further amplified—and occasionally distorted—by the overhead speakers.

I'd forgotten my gloves at home, so I alternated between clapping and burying my hands in my pockets. A great gathering of people lay between me and the distant platform. Some held up professionally made placards, others waved homemade posters. A few draped Israeli flags over their backs like capes. A number of Chabad-Lubavitchers were in attendance. These were bearded men with black suits, black ties, and short-brimmed fedoras instead of yarmulkes. There were plenty of yarmulkes as well—on plain-clothed men and boys—but the Chabad, if not the most plentiful, were clearly the most visible of the "canaries." One of the biggest applause lines came from the leader of the Anti-Defamation League, who declared, with a shake of his fist: "Whether Hasidim, Sephardic, Orthodox, or Reformed, we are all Jews. We are all brothers."

Even as I clapped with everyone else, I felt some smallness rise up in me. I couldn't help wondering just how unified we really were. Yes, everyone had closed ranks that day in a show of mutual support. We had turned out in numbers to express our shared outrage and to display our combined strength. But what kind of solidarity did that truly represent? In the long term, were the differences among these various groups more enduring than the tragedies that brought us together?

I thought about the difference between my mother's Judaism and the one I'd grown up with. In working-class Rhode Island, her Orthodox synagogue had required the women to sit upstairs while only allowing boys to receive a bar mitzvah: that all-important ritual that inducts teenagers into the responsibilities of adult Jews. At my Reformed temple in suburban Chicago, bat mitzvahs (the female version) were not only taken for granted, but the girls participated in roughly the same numbers as the boys did. My mother's exclusion from this ritual stayed with her throughout her entire life. So much so, that in 2010—at the age of seventy-two—she took fate into her own hands. Meeting with the cantor of her current temple, she underwent multiple training sessions, spent hours at home hitting "play," "pause," and "rewind" on the tape recorder, and rehearsed her reading from the Torah. At the Congregation Sukkat Shalom, in a Friday-night service before her family, friends, and other members of the synagogue, my mother stood anxiously on the bimah, overcame her terrible stage fright, and at last became a "daughter of the Commandments."

***

January in Adam Yauch Park. Stubborn vines snake their way up the concrete wall of the BQE on-ramp. Within this elevated border, a few hardy shrubs bear coarse green leaves in the shape of spears. Fistfuls of crabgrass tough it out in the dirt, while in the jungle-gym area, thin green shoots line the rubber floor mats, like short veins to nowhere. The lack of lawn makes this place feel even more barren than most other city parks—but Adam Yauch remains a park nonetheless. During the short days of winter, when headlights appear way too early on the Brooklyn-Queens Expressway, and a string of listless cars bunch together on the on-ramp, people still make their way to this playground. In thick coats and rugged boots, kids do battle with Nerf lightsabers, older siblings tug younger ones in plastic sleds. A girl sits nervously atop the tall slide of the jungle gym, which drops like a steep drawbridge many times her own height. She wants to go down but is clearly afraid. Bolstered by her father's encouragement, she finally pushes off with a shriek that's part joy, and part fear, which she hasn't yet had time to let go of.

In a few months, tight buds will form again on the trees. New leaves will speckle the branches and slowly nudge their way into the world, as springtime confers its yearly blessing on the city. New Yorkers joke about having only two and a half seasons: summer, winter, and something sandwiched in between. Soon the mild weather gives way to heat and unruly humidity, and so begins the park's most vibrant period. Pilgrims flock down Atlantic Avenue toward the waterfront, and among these, a few will peel off early and slip through the swinging gates of Adam Yauch. In summertime, no corner of this playground goes unused. Children swarm like ants over the trio of jungle gyms; hockey sticks whack the pavement between makeshift goals; and upwards of seven or eight kids vie for space around the water spigot—that strange, naked metal rod that looks abandoned by its cistern. The trees and flowering bushes are at their summer peak, and this little stitch of property, caught between an expressway and a parking garage, thrives as it must surely have been intended, when it was first conceived some seventy years ago.

What kind of place, then, does Adam Yauch Park represent? This unassuming playground that's so easy to walk right past—and so easy to dismiss in favor of nicer, greener parks in the neighborhood—somehow still attracts people from across Brooklyn and from all different backgrounds. The recreation is, for the large part, wholesome, though sometimes you'll see young couples canoodling at the stone picnic tables, their legs threaded together as their hands wander unseen. By moonlight, at those same tables, marijuana smokers pass a joint back and forth. Sometimes cyclists will ride through the playground without dismounting, in clear violation of park rules. One of those riders might confess, with some embarrassment, to miscalculating what his bladder could hold one night while returning from a nearby pub, and having to relieve himself discreetly in a hidden corner behind the bushes.

Surprisingly, in this small park with very little nature to speak of, I took one of my favorite natural photographs. It's a picture of rusted-brown leaves on the jungle-gym floor, the foliage shot through with afternoon sunlight and blazing harmonically with the red-and-yellow structure above it. I've played pickup games on both basketball courts, hit outside jumpers that I'll never replicate, missed open layups that I'll never get back. And though I vowed to give the pull-up bars a try one day, I had no interest in doing sit-ups on a solid metal bench, or in smoking a midnight joint over a stone-faced chessboard.

In a 1996 interview, Adam Yauch spoke to *Tikkun* magazine about an "us" versus "them" mentality, a destructive impulse that so often led to scapegoating. He warned that "any people, even Jews, could take a wrong turn," adding that "We must constantly keep close tabs on what we are doing and who we are becoming. And we must forgive those who have erred, just as we would hope they would forgive us." Perhaps Yauch's mixture of influences—Catholic, Jewish, and eventually Buddhist—helped him reach this understanding. The former Beastie Boy remains a perfect emblem for this modest park bearing his name, a place in which different races intersect and different religions happily coexist. The singer is a force for inspiration, a powerful addition to anyone's playlist, and a reminder of the crooked, often uncomfortable, paths we travel to reexamine our own faith.

Teaching Moments in a Time of Diaspora

On a Wednesday morning in March, just a couple days before our spring break, I met with my students for the last time. I'd asked everyone to bring their laptops for a trial "webinar," and it was a good thing we did. That first trial was a disaster. The faces on my screen kept swapping in and out in a maddening blitz, like a high-speed slide show. A screech of audio feedback sent everyone's hands over their ears, the product of so many computers huddled so closely together. Luckily, my experienced teaching assistant swooped in to save the day. She changed my viewing mode to the checkerboard layout everyone would soon grow accustomed to, and she advised my students to mute their mics when they weren't speaking. At the end of class that day, we folded our laptops with relative confidence, and we said our goodbyes with relative certainty. Everyone expected to be back on campus in a month.

It was 2020. The airwaves filled with talk of a rapidly spreading coronavirus, and many universities were hitting the pause button out of an abundance of caution. The New School had extended its spring break to two weeks, giving professors extra time to refashion their syllabi for the transition to online classes. Everyone believed this would only be temporary. It was a sign of our innocence that we all assumed a return to the physical classroom by mid-April. These were still the early days of COVID, when very little was known about the virus or its transmissibility, and when most of its damage was still occurring overseas. That damage wouldn't take long to reach our shores.

In New York City, a touch of early spring descended on my Brooklyn neighborhood. Sitting in a café on Smith Street, feeling as carefree as the pedestrians floating by, I had a hard time believing the world was coming undone. Every news report suggested as much. The World Health Organization had declared the coronavirus a global pandemic. The government of Italy had placed its entire country under quarantine. Schools were closing left and right across the United States, the NBA had suspended the rest of its season, and Broadway canceled all of its shows. Even Disneyland had shuttered the gates to its Magic Kingdom. In another week, Tokyo would postpone the Summer Olympics.

The city's first recorded COVID death came on March 1st. Within a few weeks, the virus would kill thousands of New Yorkers and leave thousands more violently ill. Patients lined hospital corridors, medical staff were getting sick or going into quarantine, and refrigerator trucks now served as temporary morgues. Both the Jacob Javits Convention Center and the Cathedral of St. John the Divine were turned into alternative care facilities. Hospital tents were erected in Central Park. A friend in radiology told me of the massive scarring he was seeing in his patients' lungs—unlike anything he'd ever witnessed before. In late March, the city's emergency dispatcher received more phone calls in a single day than it had on 9/11.

A new vocabulary took hold. Terms like "social distancing," "sheltering in place," and "flattening the curve" became the order of the day. The goal was to lower the infection rate and protect the healthcare system from collapse. My laundromat across the street closed. At every grocery store, a doorman kept a strict headcount of customers. The line for Trader Joe's circled the block like at the premiere of a Star Wars movie. Once inside, a masked greeter would squirt a thick drop of hand sanitizer into your palms, which required several seconds of rubbing to evaporate. During those first few weeks, unable to find a mask anywhere, I wrapped a winter scarf around my mouth and nose and felt my face sweating as I prowled the aisles. One day, at the fruit and vegetable market on Atlantic Avenue, I was shocked to see someone wearing an old-fashioned gas mask—the kind with eye goggles and double-barreled filters—like a refugee from the trenches of World War I.

***

On Monday, March 30th, I fired up my laptop and held my breath. I was on my own this time. The TA couldn't come to my aid—at least not in person—if anything went awry. My students had dispersed to Illinois, Maine, California, and New Mexico, among many other places. Would everyone remember to sync their watches to the East Coast? With a wave of delight, I saw the first few rectangles appear onscreen. The student names emerged above a caption that said, *"Connecting to audio…"* Those three little dots bubbled up and down suspensefully, like the flickering that preceded crew members beaming aboard the *Starship Enterprise*. With each new arrival, the existing squares shrank down and moved aside to make room, like an old biology film on cell division. Each time a new camera came on, it opened a portal into a student's private universe. I saw bedrooms that were messy beyond belief, wood-paneled basements right out of the 1970s, a funky lamp with an eye chart printed on the tall lampshade. Someone's kitchen had been taken over by a sprawling cat tower: a mini-village of perches, posts, and carpeted tunnels. Sure enough, about midway through class, a black-and-white cat named Gumdrop moseyed onscreen. On another day, we were introduced to her tortoise-shell companion, Jellybean.

After a two-week absence, it seemed important to wet our feet slowly rather than dive right into work. Did anyone have a funny anecdote to share, an interesting book to recommend? Which TV shows had they been bingeing on? It was here that I learned about the streaming Netflix series called *Tiger King*. As best I understood it, the reality show involved an unsavory man named Joe Exotic, a guy who ran an animal park by dubious, often abusive, means, and who'd supposedly put out a hit job on a rival animal collector. No thanks, I told my students: I would not be watching that one. I was a little too disgusted by the premise, and a little too afraid of getting hooked.

The April 12th return-to-school date slipped by. Classes would remain on Zoom for the rest of the semester. The decline in squares had already begun, and it wasn't long before certain students went missing more frequently or simply dropped out altogether. Even among those who were present, two or three cameras might be turned off on any given day. I found those black squares disheartening. Each one seemed a placeholder for a student who was in attendance yet somehow missing at the same time. Some individuals did speak up from their black box of obscurity, while others remained silent or were out of the room when I happened to call on them. Much as I longed for full visibility, I didn't pressure anyone to turn their camera on. You never knew what might be going on in someone's personal life, and sometimes it was simply best to leave the lights off.

Loneliness covered the country like a blanket. Penned up in our homes, we dwelled within social media and sought connection through our computer screens. I attended my first-ever online seder: a Passover table that extended virtually across the tristate area. On Facebook, friends took part in something like an old-fashioned chain letter: *Person X has nominated me to post a photo of an influential athlete—one athlete a day—for ten days. Each day I'll nominate someone else to do the same.* A similar post went around for movies and record albums. In my demographic, music by The Who, Pink Floyd, and The Beatles were par for the course, but one album took me by surprise. It showed a man in jeans and a black leather jacket with his throwing arm cocked behind his ear. In his hand was a large stone that he aimed at a mansion covered in windows. Incredibly, in one of those windows, the man's distant reflection looked like someone jamming on a guitar. This would-be hooligan was Billy Joel, and the album—*Glass Houses*—was the first record I'd ever purchased.

While half the nation sulked, the other half rose up in anger. People's theaters, gyms, and bowling alleys had been taken away from them. Parents had to juggle work with a new type of home-schooling they'd never asked for. Even as a non-viewer of *Tiger King*, I sensed that Joe Exotic's renegade mentality reflected something much larger gripping the country. A restless belligerence was brewing in people, a pent-up irritation that could no longer contain itself. That sentiment had existed prior to COVID, but the virus pushed us ever closer to the brink. The idea of uniting against a common foe gave way to a radical patriotism, one that placed personal freedom and individual choice above all else. Mask mandates, government lockdowns, and school closures were labeled un-American. Even as the death toll climbed, politicians and commentators vilified public health officials, conspiracy theorists decried public guidelines, and people in some quarters spoke openly of sacrificing seniors for the good of the economy. It was a policy that sounded eerily close to survival of the fittest.

In my Brooklyn neighborhood, I saw a similar divide between those who believed in collective action versus those who opted to fly solo. It was a common ritual among approaching strangers to either slow down on the sidewalk or steer wide of each other, usually with a courteous smile. Likewise, most people wore some kind of face covering indoors, even if improperly fastened. But there were plenty of others who floated in a bubble of oblivion or outright disregard. I was stunned to see unmasked shoppers coughing with their mouths wide open, not even a hand to shield them—as if to damn everyone else for their overprotectiveness. When supply chains faltered and grocery shelves grew thin, hoarding became a real issue. At Trader Joe's one day, I passed a guy in the depleted cereal aisle hugging four boxes to his chest, like someone taking home so many prizes at the fair. "Really?" I snapped at him, "*four* boxes?" He whipped around suddenly and stared at me with such defiance that I could only shake my head and walk away. Once, while out for an afternoon run, I was the offender to receive a stranger's scolding. I rounded a blind street corner and nearly collided with an unwitting couple, who rejected my apology and yelled in unison: "Wear a fucking mask!" Unlike the guy in the grocery store, I didn't bother turning around.

***

Sometimes my life felt relegated to the computer screen. How strange to see that mini-version of myself inside my own laptop, talking away as he stared back at me. I thought of that obnoxious boy in *Willy Wonka & the Chocolate Factory*, the loudmouth kid who zapped himself inside the TV screen and swapped his full-sized body for an avatar. Weren't we all trapped in some version of that same scenario? I suffered from online fatigue like everyone else, but I couldn't bring myself to complain about it. The virtual classroom felt like a saving grace that semester, without which we'd be relegated to the chat rooms and discussion posts from online courses of old.

Add to that the collection of tiny, amusing distractions each webinar provided. These occurred when students, forgetting they were in full view, would reposition themselves on the sofa, dig into a plate of food on their lap, or suddenly start walking from room to room—their laptop turned into a roving camera. One colleague fondly described the noise a student made while flipping through his textbook, a sound she compared to "the wind rustling a thousand leaves." Then there was the student I called on while she sat sideways and was clearly preoccupied with someone offscreen. The student fessed up immediately. She was doing her sister's nails, and the whole class was impressed by the bright-red extensions, like a row of painted pistachio shells, which her sister showed off to the camera.

Those nails weren't the only thing to defy nature. I was accustomed to seeing my students hesitate mid-sentence, but it was something else to see them freeze in place altogether. At any given moment, someone might become a still-life portrait of themselves, even as their voice carried on for another few seconds. Their words turned jittery and bionic until their dying thought was vacuumed up like the person speaking. So the checkerboard would rearrange itself. So the vanished student would resurface again a few moments later, in a different location. One day during a Wi-Fi outage, I was forced to dial in by phone and lead discussion in what felt like a prolonged version of blind-man's bluff.

Even as we battened down the hatches, surprising buds of hope sprang up. In the United States, not a single school shooting took place during the month of March, the first such absence in March in almost two decades. Reduced traffic led to dramatic improvements in air quality around the world, such as in Kathmandu, Nepal, where people could see Mt. Everest for the first time in a generation. Someone reported dolphins in the cleaner-running canals of Venice, a story that, though quickly debunked, nevertheless captured everyone's imagination. It made us believe that we could still, if we put our minds to it, reverse some of the terrible damage we'd wrought upon our planet.

One April afternoon, foiled by the long line outside Key Food, I turned around and started back home when an oncoming runner suddenly veered toward me and stopped. I recognized her right away She was a former student of mine and a stand-up comedian. I'd seen her just the year before, when she headlined at a comedy club in the East Village. On the sidewalk we maintained a few feet of distance as she told me her COVID story. Cut off from her audience, unable to tour, she'd been going stir-crazy until she started a podcast with a fellow comedian. The show was called *2 Non Doctors*, and together they kibitzed on a range of health issues, from dyslexia to depression to a bizarre condition called Misophonia. Misophonia was *not*—as her comedian friend joked—the fear of being a "Miss" instead of a "Mrs." The word literally meant a hatred of sound, and it produced—at least in her friend—irrational fits of rage over little things like gum chewing, pen clicking, or even mindless hair twirling. Hearing this, I could only imagine what storm would erupt had she been a student in my colleague's class—and been subjected each day to the page-turner's rustling of a thousand leaves.

***

The spring semester bumped along. Students lost their jobs as waiters, hostesses, and baristas, with no way to plug the financial hole. In spite of the strain they all felt, my remaining students managed to pull themselves across the finish line. In my Culture & Conflict class, they wrote on an array of contemporary issues portrayed in films and TV shows, such as mental illness in the movie *The Joker* or depression in the animated series *BoJack Horseman*. (To my disappointment, no one wrote about *Tiger King*.) In my Coming of Age Short Fiction class, some students wrote traditional essays while others led a pretend therapy session with a few main characters, who were united around a common theme or shared struggle.

These were younger protagonists, but I'd come to observe that those early, formative issues often stuck around through adulthood. The tension between honoring our parents and questioning their judgment persists into our later years, and that tightrope became a lot harder to walk during the pandemic. Fortunately, my parents had sailed into old age without serious health issues, but during COVID they struck me as elderly for the first time. In our video chats I was startled by the gray hair pushing up from my mother's roots, trying to reclaim what she could no longer color at the salon. (The gray was less visible in my father's comb-over.) Even more disturbing was the decline in my mother's memory. She grew furious when the maid stopped coming on Fridays, accusing my father of making the decision unilaterally. This was the default setting in their marriage, except that in this case, my father had not only discussed it with her beforehand but had reminded her more than once.

My dad became entrenched in his own way. A retired cardiologist, he scoured the daily infection rates by city, county, and state, scrutinizing the trends and leading off each conversation with the latest stats. He went shopping at 6:30 a.m., right when the story opened, and he refused to take my mother outside for walks. That led to heated arguments between us, as I charged him with turning Mom into a shut-in. Safety was one thing, irrationality another. How else to explain his abrupt reversal in returning to the hair salon? I nearly blew a gasket when I found out. Why would he put the two of them at risk over something so inessential, I demanded? "We can't stop breathing!" he fired back, with no acknowledgment of the clear contradiction.

I took some relief from the salon manager, who told me they'd installed an air purifier and were only admitting two customers at a time. And I took great comfort, I have to admit, when I saw both parents again in our next video chat, the two of them sitting side by side with their brown hair fully restored.

Everyone felt an aching desire to return to normal. With the warmer weather, death rates were falling in New York and the city went through a phased reopening. But previously spared states like Texas and Florida were now being ravaged, and the nationwide death toll topped one hundred thousand. Then, as the start of summer approached, a giant hammer came down across the land. In Minneapolis, a Black man named George Floyd was apprehended for passing a counterfeit twenty-dollar bill, and as he lay face down and handcuffed, a policeman kneeled on the back of his neck. "*I can't breathe*," Floyd muttered, while the policeman and his fellow officers looked on passively. For nine-plus minutes, Floyd repeated the same plea in softer, ever-beseeching tones, until at some point he quietly expired.

Bystander video spread around the world. Demonstrations erupted in over 140 cities across the United States. Most of these were peaceful, but a small contingent of criminals smashed windows, robbed businesses, and became violent. In Brooklyn, demonstrations near the Barclays Center led to clashes with police, scores of arrests, the use of pepper spray, and a citywide curfew of 11 p.m.—which was quickly changed to 8 p.m. Nighttime sirens became a constant, as did the buzz of patrolling helicopters. I went to a midday rally at Cadman Plaza, the same site as the *No Hate. No Fear.* rally I'd attended five months earlier, after an anti-Semitic attack north of the city. The rules of social distancing were not strictly observed that day. Chants of "No Justice, No Peace" rippled across the plaza. Shouts of "Black Lives Matter" were followed by rhythmic clapping. The most powerful moment came when hundreds of people dropped to one knee and raised a fist in the air, as a call and response began. "Say His Name?... George Floyd. Say His Name?... George Floyd." The shouts echoed throughout Cadman Plaza. The collective cry carried on for several moments, as people gave voice to a man who'd been brutally and permanently robbed of his own.

Uncertainty lingered through the summer and fall. In July I rented a one-month sublet close to my parents' house, only to discover, on the day before my flight, that the property manager was unreachable. His phone number was no longer in service, and the money I'd sent the guy was unrecoverable. I felt the bitter sting of all those Craigslist warnings about wire fraud, having thought myself too smart to be anyone's target. I flew home anyway, found an Airbnb that was equally close, and breathed a whole lot easier when my post-flight COVID test came back negative.

In November, as the death toll passed the number of all American casualties from World War I, we voted out of office the president who'd once called COVID a hoax and suggested people inject themselves with bleach. Two months later, the new year brought a trio of COVID vaccines that became a blessing for so many, reuniting families and promising a light at the end of the tunnel. For anti-vaxxers, it turned into another call to arms and a continuation of the fight for personal freedom. The unvaccinated would die in disproportionate numbers, but even the vaccinated continued to get sick. New variants emerged, the country limped slowly toward convalescence, but eventually, after enough time, the coronavirus finally began to loosen its grip.

When the doors to school reopened, a fair number of students still slipped through the cracks. Attendance rose and fell, our classrooms remained a sponge for so much discord circulating in the world, and yet we somehow made it through that first semester. Then we got through the next one. COVID drove home the hard truth that teachers spend much of their lives trying to reject: You can't defend every student against risk, just like you can't protect every person against infection. But

COVID also reminded us—teachers, students, and everyone else—of what's most essential in who we are. It highlighted the very human need we all have to express ourselves, to exist in a public space, and to feel like we're not alone in the world.

A Tale of Two Catastrophes

On a late Wednesday morning in July, with the temperature hovering close to ninety degrees, a caravan of police motorcycles revved their engines and slowly proceeded up Broadway. They began near the old Trinity Church in lower Manhattan, while a half-block behind them, traveling at a snail's pace, came a vintage black convertible with whitewall tires, chrome racing stripe, and the city seal emblazoned on its side. Thousands of spectators cheered on the plain-clothed woman sitting on the trunk. The woman faced forward with her feet perched on the backseat upholstery, turning her head from sidewalk to sidewalk as she waved to her adoring fans. On any other day, the majority of those fans would never have even recognized her. That was the whole point. On that particular July morning, in her role as grand marshal of the Hometown Heroes Parade, Sandra Lindsay was being honored as a nurse from Queens, an essential worker during the pandemic, and the country's first recipient of the COVID vaccine.

This dedication of floats and marching bands, of bagpipes and confetti, was meant to celebrate those who'd helped the city pull through the first year of the coronavirus. The participants included first responders, healthcare workers, educators, grocery store clerks, pharmacy staff, transit employees, and so many others. The parade began only a few blocks from the 9/11 Memorial and Museum—and just a couple months before the twentieth anniversary of September 11th. On that day, the city would commemorate another tragedy that dealt a terrible blow to the soul of New Yorkers, and that tested its resolve in ways that felt profoundly similar to the COVID-19 pandemic.

It was 2021. Almost two decades had passed since the attack on the World Trade Center. Many of us still considered that event the tragedy of our time, even though the day had receded in the minds of so many others. The once-common bumper sticker—9/11 NEVER FORGET—rarely turned up on cars anymore, and when it did, there was usually a corner peeled off or the letters looked washed out. It wasn't just the message that had faded: So, too, had the good will it once stood for. The idea of everyone pulling together in a moment of crisis—the belief that IF YOU SEE SOMETHING, SAY SOMETHING—had been turned upside-down. In its place, a great many Americans either intentionally looked away from disaster, or they simply wouldn't accept what their own eyes told them.

I'd come to the parade by way of the 5 train, from Union Square. After eight and a half years in Brooklyn, I'd jumped the East River back to Manhattan. My search for a new home had brought the usual ups and downs, the same inventory of headaches and sorrows—plus another installment of The Apartment That Got Away. Off and on the hunt had continued, only to stall again for several months. A few more seasons came and went, then COVID made a mess of everything. When my search resumed in the fall of 2020, I wandered into a rare phenomenon in New York City: a buyers' market.

That long search would come to a head a few months later. In the first week of January, a mix of very good and very bad fortune came together on the same day. I'd lined up a couple of strong contenders to visit one afternoon: a studio apartment in Chelsea and another studio on Third Avenue near Union Square. The date was January 6th. It was the same day Congress was set to certify the November presidential election. Only one thing stood in the way: The losing president had yet to concede. After sixty defeats in court, the outgoing president had switched to a break-glass strategy: bring his supporters to Washington, DC—and make sure they brought the heat. "Be there, it will be wild," he'd urged them, and since then a growing menace had taken shape around those words. The threats and angry rhetoric by election deniers had gotten so bad that a Republican senator from Nebraska rebuked his own party, saying: "Adults don't point a loaded gun at the heart of legitimate self-government."

On January 6th, I rode the 2 train from Brooklyn Borough Hall to 23rd Street and Seventh Avenue, on Manhattan's West Side. I would visit the Chelsea studio by myself and then meet my broker at the studio near Union Square. After exiting the subway at street level, I saw nothing unusual in the flow of traffic. There was no indication on the people's faces that the day had already gone sideways. My cell phone rang just then. Without a word of hello, my friend from the East Village asked if I was paying attention to all the craziness. I assumed he meant the president's rally, and I told him that I simply didn't care anymore. I began a rant about how sickened I was by the whole thing, but before I could pick up steam my friend cut me off.

"Jonathan, the Capitol's been stormed," he said.

Stormed? What did he mean, *stormed?*

He meant that the barricades had been overrun and protestors were now mobbing the building.

I flew into a rage right there on Seventh Avenue. I became one of those angry cell phone talkers that people stared at and purposely steered clear of. I hoped that motherf—r was happy, I yelled, he'd gotten exactly what he wanted. For a few more blocks we talked (my friend talked, I shouted), until I reached the address on 25th Street and found the seller's broker waiting outside. I didn't have to tell him anything: He'd been getting texts nonstop from his friends and family in Washington. Some woman was bleeding, he told me—though he couldn't say who or why. Once in the apartment I kept glancing at my phone for updates, and our conversation kept swinging back to what was happening in DC. It felt like some alternative reality. I was wandering through a stranger's apartment, opening and closing kitchen cabinets, sizing up closet space, glancing around half-heartedly, while just a couple hundred miles away, the Congress of the United States was under siege.

So promising in its online photographs, the Chelsea studio was neither as nice nor well-lit in person. I told the agent I'd think about it, and then I stepped outside into the increasing gray of afternoon. With a cold January sun at my back, I walked the cheerless streets in a fog of disbelief. The thing that was happening couldn't be happening. The thing that was happening was a complete outrage. My broker, when I met him at the second building, told me he hadn't seen any footage either, so neither of us knew the grim nature of the battle taking place. The protestors wielded flagpoles as spears, they struck Capitol police officers with the blunt end of fire extinguishers, rammed them with metal barricades. They subjected the police to tasers, bear spray, and the brute force of their own seized riot shields. The only thing more unimaginable than the weapons themselves was the deep malice in the rioters who used them.

"Forget it," said my broker, when I described the other studio, "this doesn't sound like the one for you." Michael was a rare breed of real estate agent. He wouldn't let me take something just to get the search over with—or just to pocket his commission sooner. In that second apartment, he tagged along patiently as I took photographs and shot videos of the layout. I asked questions of the seller's agent, which Michael followed up with sharper and much more informed queries of his own. Afterward, in our subway ride back to Brooklyn, we held a frank conversation. The studio was spacious, well located, and priced fairly low for the neighborhood, but the walls would need repainting, the floors refinishing, and I was already at the upper range of what I could afford.

"Go home and give it some thought," he said, without tipping his hand. That night, I stewed over the pros and cons in my mind. I weighed the spacious living area and galley kitchen against the scratched floors and blemished gray walls, plus the cost and effort involved in fixing them both. I crunched the numbers again and again, sought the advice of a couple close friends, and finally went to sleep on it. By morning, my mind had been made up. I called Michael to give him the green light, and he went to work on a strategy that would land me—after several months, and several rigorous steps—in my new home.

Long before then, and hours before I'd come to my decision, the National Guard arrived at the Capitol. Three hours after the fighting began, an FBI SWAT team worked with other security forces to clear out the ransacked building. Astonishingly few arrests were made, while the people still parading around the defiled chamber were treated with kid gloves. Much later that night, when Congress reassembled, more than a hundred Republican House members and several of their senate colleagues—all of whom had fled for their safety earlier that day—voted against certification. Deliberations turned heated as they dragged into the wee hours. The chamber nearly came to blows when a Democratic House member publicly denounced the election deniers, calling them liars and blaming them for the violence. A few Republicans rose from their chairs and started toward the center aisle. A handful of Democrats did likewise. The speaker gaveled down hard and called the House to order, the sergeant at arms rushed to intervene, and fisticuffs were narrowly avoided.

***

Following the parade up Broadway, I tagged along for several blocks behind the Walgreens float. Every few minutes, the rear porthole would shoot up colorful bursts of confetti, turning Broadway into a remarkable scene like an impressionist painting. Each new eruption brought another roar from the crowd. They cheered again for the police marching band, the union workers, and the nurses in their various-colored scrubs. To the west of us, I kept seeing the smooth glass monolith of the Freedom Tower. At that moment, I was working on an essay about the twentieth anniversary of September 11th, and even amid the pageantry and loud music, my thoughts kept merging with memories of those attacks. I got emotional thinking about the flood of dust-covered refugees from lower Manhattan, the photographs of all the missing around the city, the football players who held hands and cried during the national anthem. I got emotional remembering those dozen firefighters I had seen in Grand Central Station, only six days after 9/11, when a crowd of thousands parted suddenly and the entire Main Concourse erupted with applause.

I grew emotional thinking about a photo of the North Tower in mid-collapse. Snapped from my roof deck, the picture contained a secret that only revealed itself years later, when I scanned the negative and could see a larger image onscreen. The North Tower descends in a terrible fountain of rubble. Humongous clouds of smoke surge upward to choke out a portion of the sky. In the foreground, the patchwork of roof decks have all been vacated—all of them except one: the roof deck directly across the street from me. On a tiny island above the city, two women stand front to back with their heads turned away from the falling tower. The taller woman in front seems petrified. Her body is ramrod-straight, her arms flat at her sides like a Navy SEAL diver. The other woman hugs her from behind, her arms encircling her companion in what looks like the Heimlich maneuver. I can almost hear her whispering—*Don't look. Don't look. Don't look…*—and I can almost feel one woman's heart breaking in the other's arms.

On that hot July morning, standing among the parade goers, I was reminded of 9/11 in the best way. Like the first responders of twenty years ago, these essential workers had helped lift up a city that was brought to its knees. And yet something had clearly changed since then. A sickness was spreading throughout the country: a condition that went beyond COVID and had been around much longer. It infected the way we responded to mass shootings, election lies, even the pandemic itself. Did anyone embody that sickness more strongly than the person most widely revered after September 11th? A few weeks after the Hometown Heroes Parade, he and I would cross paths in a brief encounter that embarrassed me at the time, and that I've continued to regret ever since.

Twenty years ago, Rudy Giuliani's place in history had seemed secure. In the days after September 11th, rattled by his escape from the command center under the North Tower, he lost his trademark bluster and became a nationwide figure of reassurance. For his special combination of strength and vulnerability, he'd earned the nickname "America's Mayor"—a title he might've taken to his grave if not for his precipitous fall. As an advisor to the defeated president, he'd demeaned himself by voicing wild conspiracy theories, staging bizarre stunts like a press conference next to a sex shop, and bumbling through scenes of leaking hair dye and public flatulence. He'd turned into a tragic buffoon—but a dangerous buffoon nonetheless. At the Ellipse rally on January 6th, in those crucial moments before the riot began, Giuliani called for a "trial by combat" and poured more fuel onto an already inflamed mob. In the ensuing months, he'd seen his law license suspended in New York State, his drinking openly ridiculed, and his celebrity reduced to selling online birthday and bar mitzvah greetings.

Late July rolled around. I was biking up Third Avenue through Midtown, headed to a tennis date in Central Park, when my attention flashed upon someone familiar. I'd sped past without a good look, but the long face, large sloping forehead, and round glasses called out to me with a strange singularity. Had I imagined it? I couldn't let go without knowing for sure, so I waited for the light to turn red and then circled back against the one-way traffic. Lo and behold, it was him. Just a few feet from the curb stood Rudy Giuliani, wearing dark slacks and a light-blue button-down. His eyes were glued to his cell phone, and a couple of handlers, I noticed this time around, were also keeping him company.

A wire of excitement ran through me. How many times had I rehearsed this scenario in my head? In the version I'd scripted, I would walk right up to the man and say, "Mr. Giuliani, I was in New York on September 11th, I watched from my roof deck as the towers burned, and I just wanted to thank you for your great leadership and humanity that day. Mr. Mayor—" I would add, in the exact same tone of humility, "—our country sorely misses that man, and we desperately need him back." Before he could answer, I would turn and make a smooth exit, persuading myself that a surprise olive branch from a well-meaning stranger might inspire the man, however slightly, to some kind of personal awakening.

It was magical thinking, of course. As the sidewalk drew closer, my legs shook nervously and those eloquent words fractured in my mind. His two handlers suddenly loomed a lot larger, and I felt my grip loosening on the handbrakes. The bike picked up speed again, and as I skirted past him the words leapt out of me in an uncontrolled spasm: "Hey *R-u-u-d-y!*" His face jerked up, his eyes made a quick assessment of me, and he looked right back down at his cell phone. Even as my bike arced away from him, I already debated looping around again. I wanted to take another crack at it, but my nerves were still unsettled, and I remembered my tennis date in Central Park. (It was a first date, I should mention.) In the middle of Third Avenue, in that flickering moment of indecision, I saw the light turn green again, and I quickly scooted aside as a pack of cars came racing toward me.

It was over—I had blown my opportunity. There was no way to reset the table, no way to win back whatever good will

I might've achieved. With a wounded pride I joined the flow of traffic uptown, fleeing the scene like one more anonymous heckler. For the rest of that afternoon, and for a long time to come, I would be haunted by my own absurd behavior that day, and my own great failure to meet the moment.

PART FOUR

The City of Yesterday and Tomorrow

Pastrami and Wry

When I moved to New York in 1998, one of the great debates among people who lived downtown was where to get the best pastrami: Second Avenue Deli or Katz's. To me, it was never really much of a competition. The sandwich at Katz's was both heartier and more affordable ($8.25 versus $10.75—a sizable difference to a graduate student), while the environments at each place couldn't have been more different. Second Avenue Deli fancied itself a proper restaurant, where a host walked you to your table and handed you a plastic-coated menu, and your pastrami came delivered in a tidy, well-composed sandwich. Katz's was just the opposite. From a corner entrance you passed through a turnstile and were handed a small ticket stub before you waded into the sprawling circus of a cafeteria. An extended counter ran along the right-hand side, where customers crowded into several lines with endpoints nearly impossible to ascertain. Thereafter, you were on your own. You navigated the swarm until you found the best line to stand in, and then you watched with envy as the customers ahead of you placed their orders.

The magic happened in plain sight. On the opposite side of a glass partition, the slicer speared a pitchfork utensil into a ham-sized slab of pastrami, its black exterior a rub of mixed spices. Using his long serrated knife, he carved off lovely pink shavings that fell one by one onto a clean white saucer. The first two chunks went on a separate plate, which he hoisted atop the partition so you could whet your appetite (and leave a tip in the tip cup). When the shaggy pink meat formed a heaping pile, he stopped his bladework and assembled the pieces inside two slices of rye bread that looked too thin to handle the load. Next came a plateful of pickles, medium- and dark-green, which he quartered into spears and served with the sandwich on a brown tray. Your ticket stub was marked and returned, you backed away carefully through the waiting customers, and you hunted for an open table before your sandwich turned cold.

Even if it had been a closer call between delis, another factor would've tipped the scales in favor of Katz's. The deli on the corner of Ludlow and Houston Street was the same one my grandfather used to go to as a child: the same deli he'd eventually take my father to as a young boy. This was in the early 1940s. It was a time when elevated trains covered much of Manhattan, when my father's family still lived near my grandfather's drugstore in Midtown, and when my grandparents occasionally brought my dad to his father's old neighborhood on the Lower East Side.

These stories had washed over me during my own childhood. In suburban Chicago, I grew up hearing tales about daily life in Pickwick Pharmacy, so named because of the Pickwick Arms Hotel down the street; about my father's fabulous adventures at the 1939 World's Fair; and about Mayor La Guardia reading the funnies over the radio during the delivery-truck strike. That era felt largely removed from my own, and yet even on the North Shore of Chicago, I still saw living reminders of the past. An elevated subway train—like my father's beloved

Second Avenue El—traveled from my hometown of Wilmette into the heart of the city. Two stories high, the El tracks shuttled between rooftops and billboards, with the train making stops at mysterious-named stations like Jarvis, Granville, and Bryn Mawr. The train took you right past Wrigley Field—a ballpark as beautiful and majestic as that other famous stadium in the Bronx. The El went all the way to the downtown Loop, where it roamed like a centipede at the feet of giant office buildings. Chicago had celebrated its own world's fair—the 1893 Columbian Exposition—whose legacy persisted in buildings like the Art Institute, the Museum of Science and Industry, and several other glorious stone structures. And yet of all the restaurants I'd been to in Chicagoland, and all the delis I'd ever heard about, none bore any resemblance to the bustling delicatessen from my father's past, let alone the Jewish neighborhood to which it belonged.

On his trips to Katz's, my dad always ordered "the special." It was nothing more than a kosher beef hot dog, which he ate with a side of French fries and a Doctor Brown's Cel-Ray soda. Those all-beef kosher dogs were in abundance where I grew up, so it seemed to me a wasted trip to pass on the more extravagant pastrami or corned beef. Years later, when I moved to New York and started making my own pilgrimages to the Lower East Side, most of the Jews had long since abandoned the neighborhood, while the smaller shop owners were steadily being pushed out by swank bars and fancy restaurants. And yet an aura of my father's past still clung to the area. Tiny synagogues dotted Stanton Street, Rivington Street, and the intersecting side streets. Russ & Daughters, the old family proprietor of smoked fish and pickled herring, still did a strong business. And on the corner of Houston and Ludlow, only two subway stops from where I lived, the sign for Katz's Deli still loomed like a beacon from my father's time. In the front window, those giant hanging salamis stood like proud talismans of the old world.

On a wintry night in February 2023, I went to Katz's for the first time since before the pandemic. A friend from the Village came with me. In the before-times, we would often split a sandwich (a half sandwich at Katz's was a meal unto itself) and share a plate of their giant wedge fries. Afterward, stuffed and lethargic, we would walk a couple blocks to a place called Two-Bit's Retro Arcade, a combination bar and classic video arcade on Essex Street, where my friend played Ms. Pac-Man and I made a beeline for Donkey Kong. Unfortunately, Two-Bit's had been a casualty of COVID, so we now had to troop all the way up to Barcade, on St. Mark's Place, if we wanted to give our fingers a workout.

Katz's had not only weathered the pandemic but seemed to be thriving better than ever. This was evident in the half-block line along the sidewalk, in the dining tables that were jam-packed, and in the dollar amount I found scribbled on my ticket stub after ordering. For some reason, I had frozen the cost of pastrami at a pre-COVID rate of $18.25. The going rate was now $24.45 (another reason my friend and I often went fifty-fifty). Why should that have surprised me? The laws of nature applied as rigidly to Katz's Deli as they did to Manhattan real estate. A bad economy might temporarily flatten prices, but they would rise, unfailingly, over the course of time.

After my friend and I had divided up the wedge fries and sandwich halves, I snapped a photo before digging in. Imagine a beautiful mountain of pastrami held in place by two mittens of rye bread; a pile of large French fries stacked together like freshly sawed lumber; a row of canoe-shaped pickles neatly aligned on a white dish; and in the corner of the tray, a can of Dr. Brown's soda with its old-timey label. I texted the photo with a heart emoji to my father, who would know exactly where I was. Then my feast began. I cracked a bite of a half-sour pickle. I chomped the crispy edge of a French fry, whose potato filling was way too hot, so I quickly cooled my tongue with a sip of Cel-Ray soda. My cell phone chirped—it was my father's reply—and I anticipated his standard response about getting "the special." Because of my extended absence from Katz's, I couldn't help hoping for just a little more this time. Instead, I got even less. "Be careful," my dad wrote, "COVID is still rampant." That was it. There was no follow-up message, no reference to where I was or the picture I'd sent. Not even a quick: "Enjoy your dinner."

With irked fingers I started typing a reply, but then I reversed my thumbs and deleted it. What was the point in scolding him? After all my years of living in New York, and all my years of being an adult, I was still trying to close the distance between us. I continued to believe I could layer his past onto the present: that the two of us could forge new memories as durable as his old ones. But the past and present rarely fit together neatly. Even during his visits to New York, we had trouble tuning to the same wavelength. My father carried around his history wherever we went, and he was always ready to unpack it. In restaurants, he liked to educate the waitstaff about which elevated trains used to pass nearby, what years they'd been torn down, and what personal connections he'd had to the neighborhood. These stories impressed strangers and were amusing to his family as well—until the habit became a calling card at every meal. More frustrating to me was his insistence on referring to subways by their maiden names. Instead of saying the N/R/W or the A/C/E, he would rattle off terms like "the IRT" or "the BMT" (the Interborough Rapid Transit or the Brooklyn-Manhattan Transit). It was like some foreigner who expected you to understand the metric system, and it guaranteed that any effort to make plans would begin with a maddening exercise in translation.

Family trips brought the usual family baggage. When my father wasn't moored to the past, his mind tended to fast-forward to whatever came next on the agenda and how soon we would get there. Living in the moment proved especially difficult for him. At meals he would hunt down the waitress with his eyes as he waited to order, and once again after he'd finished eating. Sometimes you could feel his impatience churning beneath the surface; other times it agitated beyond his control. That was the case one summer afternoon in the Village, when we'd purchased movie tickets a half hour early and then argued about where to spend the time. My mother and I wanted to wait in a nearby café with air-conditioning, while my father preferred the hot, empty lobby of the theater—even though there was no risk of not getting good seats. He followed us outside for a half block, but he kept on grumbling until a public feud ignited. One family member told the other to shut up, the other person yelled before storming off, and the sidewalk diners were treated to a small piece of cinema free of charge.

Thankfully, the moments of connection arrived as well. During my many years in the Village and Brooklyn Heights, my parents and I took numerous walks through both neighborhoods, we visited Central Park and the Brooklyn Botanic Gardens, and they even came to a couple of readings I gave. In 2016, I joined them in Morningside Heights for my father's sixty-year reunion at Columbia, where he and a few classmates gave talks on various topics of history or nostalgia. Biased or not, I can confidently attest that none of the other talks resonated as strongly as my father's. He reprised an old piece he'd written for the Chicago Literary Club, an account of his boyhood visit to the 1939 World's Fair in Queens. Describing its two iconic monuments—the Trylon and Perisphere—he spoke as if they were the Eighth and Ninth Wonders of the World. He gushed about the General Motors and Ford pavilions, the children's ride called Trip Around the World, and the giant panoramic display of the City of the Future.

This last exhibit, belonging to the World of Tomorrow, offered a massive architectural model of an urban landscape. It was a utopian city that proliferated with skyscrapers, overhead walkways, and curving highways that my dad called "ribbons of perfection." My father had just turned eighty the month before, and yet you'd have thought—from his starry expression and many vivid portrayals—that he'd attended the fair only a couple days earlier.

A few years after this fantastical childhood experience, my dad's family had left their apartment in Midtown and moved closer to those fairgrounds, in the Forest Hills section of Queens. In all his visits over the years, he'd shown no interest in seeing that old neighborhood. I had my own suspicions why. From my trips to LaGuardia Airport, my rides on the R train to an old girlfriend in Astoria, and a long-ago visit to my aging grandmother, I had a well-established view of the borough. Here was a place of giant thoroughfares, charmless commercial streets, and cookie-cutter houses pushed together on tight-fitting lots. Or so I'd come to believe. Nearly two decades after arriving in New York, I would discover a section of the city unlike any other I'd seen before.

Why had my father pitched this impromptu visit? His sudden desire to see Forest Hills again was no clearer to me than whatever impulse had long opposed it. As we exited the F train, the ugly sprawl of Queens Boulevard quickly confirmed my previous impressions. And yet, within a few short blocks, everything changed. The sprawl melted away as the borough transformed itself into something resembling a leafy suburb of Westchester. How could this be? I saw gorgeous mansions of brick and stone, traditional houses with picture windows and large front porches, mission-style homes with Spanish roofs. I kept turning my head in disbelief. Had the area always been this way, I asked my father? Yes, it had, he answered. I started laughing. "What a con job!" I said. I felt like someone who'd had a prank pulled on him. Not that my dad had ever claimed poverty, but I'd always viewed his childhood through the lens of the Depression, through his immigrant-named friends like Angelo and Achille, his family move from Manhattan to a far-out section of Queens, and that dim brown apartment building where my grandmother had lived. None of this pointed to the pristine, suburban-style riches I now encountered.

Amid these attractive houses and spacious lawns, my dad took us to what used to be PS 3 (Public School 3), now renamed PS 303. It was the site of a banner moment in my father's childhood. At the age of eleven, playing stickball with his friends, he'd swung his bat just right and connected with the sweet spot of the pink rubber ball. The Spaldeen—as those balls were nicknamed—went flying out of the schoolyard, over and across the street, and smack into the chimney of a tall brick mansion. It was a distance none of his peers had ever reached, at least as far as my dad remembered. He told me this without quite bragging, but with a touch of the same pride I heard in the other facts and trivia he often recited. None of which came anywhere close to being in the same category, not as far as I was concerned. Not even his score on an IQ test would have impressed me more. My pride in that moment might've equaled what my father himself was feeling, though neither of us could match the feeling of triumph in that eleven-year-old boy, who stood on these same grounds decades earlier and watched as his pink rubber ball sailed high over the schoolyard, across 110th Street, and beyond the limits of his own imagination.

I returned to Katz's Deli in April of 2023, this time by myself. I'd celebrated my birthday the night before, so on my actual birth date I found myself alone at a place called Pause Café, a half block south of Houston on Clinton Street. I'd arrived in the late afternoon to catch up on some journal writing, and by the time I put my pen down, the sun had faded and a nighttime crowd had overtaken the café. I packed up my things and exited with no destination in mind. So rarely did I visit the Lower East Side anymore that I decided to wander around and soak up a bit more of the neighborhood. The streets had changed dramatically. Rows of wood-frame cabanas, erected during COVID, lined many of the sidewalks, creating a raucous environment of open-air drinking and dining. That ambience seemed to capture much of the Lower East Side, although occasionally, here and there, I would stumble on a tamer block that felt pleasantly removed from the circus atmosphere. It was in these moments that I contemplated the neighborhood as it used to be, in the days of my father and grandfather.

Many of the hallmarks were still there. I saw them in the slash of a fire escape across a prewar building; in the dim stone carvings of a former tenement; in the darkened stained glass of a narrow synagogue, hiding its colors within. I felt nostalgic for an era I'd been no part of but still felt some distant claim to, as if my family history had been laminated onto my own. At Rivington Street, feeling awash in sentiment, I texted my dad to ask if he knew the cross streets of where my grandfather had lived. His reply came immediately. Norfolk between Stanton and Rivington, he believed. Rivington had been my grandfather's stop on the Second Avenue El, he told me, but because he didn't know my grandfather's precise childhood address, I couldn't verify whether his old apartment was still standing or had been torn down, like the Midtown pharmacy he once owned.

It was getting later, I felt myself getting hungrier, and yet I still chose not to hop on a Citi Bike and ride home. My feet must've known their destination long before I did. They arrived at the intersection of Houston and Ludlow, where I joined the line outside the corner entrance, slipped past the turnstile just inside the door, and carried my ticket stub to the waiting congregation by the deli counter.

The woman in front of me was towing a wheeled suitcase, and I asked her jokingly if she'd come straight from the airport. "Yes," she answered, without batting an eye. She was German, I found out, and during her long layover at JFK she'd commuted into the city specifically for Katz's pastrami.

How had she known about Katz's, I asked her?

She was a chef, and it turned out that Katz's was well known in her community. "Before here, I went to Joey's pizza," she said. I scratched my head and thought about this. Did she mean *Joe's* Pizza in the West Village?

Yes, that's the one!" The small take-out near Bleecker and Sixth Avenue was considered by many to serve the best slices in the city. That reputation had apparently reached all the way to Germany.

At my turn to order, I did a double-take of the overhead menu on the back wall. The cost of pastrami was now $25.95: a dollar fifty more than just a couple months earlier. That wasn't the only change they'd made. Katz's didn't serve half sandwiches anymore, although they did offer a combination half sandwich with soup. Thus did I walk away from the counter with a still-impressive plate of pastrami and a matzoh ball soup with the single largest matzoh ball I'd ever seen. Each trip to Katz's felt like a feast for the ages, and I once again marked the occasion with a photograph. I couldn't resist sending it to my father: my latest digital postcard. On the center plate, pink slabs of pastrami huddled beneath a hood of rye bread. On a smaller side dish, pickle spears lay side by side like a row of sardines. Next to this, sitting in a pool of dark brown broth, an enormous matzoh ball crested twice as high as the bowl's rim.

This time, my father didn't disappoint. He responded in short order, making his usual quip about "the special" (*Did they still serve it?*). It was a brief but gratifying exchange, especially when combined with our previous texts about my grandfather. I realized that it was up to me to temper my own expectations. Even though I hungered for a little more feeling in his dialogue, or simply a little more dialogue itself, I still believed in the greater sum of what our correspondence amounted to. Each text message we shared—like each bite of pastrami—added another link to the larger family chain. Each of those links extended the generational bond across space, time, and the perpetual long lines at Katz's Deli.

Hello (And Goodbye) To All That

People who keep notebooks are a different breed altogether, lonely and resistant rearrangers of things, anxious malcontents, children afflicted apparently at birth with some presentiment of loss.

–Joan Didion

I SPENT MY FIRST TWO WEEKS in New York sleeping on a friend's sofa in Greenwich Village. This was in August 1998. My friend wasn't from the city either, but she'd been here long enough to think that anyone who stayed beyond five years would likely remain for the long haul. A few years later, and well beyond that five-year mark, she herself would leave New York for her native West Coast. She wasn't the only one. Other people who'd been here much longer—friends or colleagues who'd seemed to purchase an unlimited subway card—decided to pull up stakes and move on. Some left for a better opportunity elsewhere, others because a better opportunity had come their spouse's way. Some moved to be closer to family, others because they'd started a family of their own. There was no pattern to where they ended up—Colorado, Texas, upstate New York—except for one thing they all shared: None of them seemed to look back afterward.

In her essay "Goodbye to All That," Joan Didion describes the glowing life of a transplant in New York City, but also how those intense fires eventually burn out. She notes the feeling that any newcomer to Manhattan will instantly recognize: the anticipation that "something extraordinary would happen any minute, any day, any month," and that the extraordinary could be lurking right around the corner. In an impression of F. Scott Fitzgerald, she refers to New York as "an infinitely romantic notion, the mysterious nexus of all love and money and power." And yet—as if taking another cue from the author of *The Great Gatsby*—she undercuts this same vision by calling New York "the shining and perishable dream itself." What is it that makes that dream perishable? To read Didion, you can't help wondering if a city paved with such high expectations will inevitably lead to disappointment, as if those dreams come prepackaged with an expiration date.

As a young writer floating through a world of cocktail parties, fashionable restaurants, and glamorous acquaintances, Didion never stopped feeling as if she were on some "extended leave" from real life. There was something too incredible about the experience—so much so that she kept anticipating the curtain would fall at any moment. Eight years later, it finally did. The nagging unreality seemed to have finally caught up with her, and Didion realized that "the golden rhythm was broken." In a different essay ("On Keeping a Notebook"), she describes feeling profoundly jaded as she rode the subway, saying: "I noticed for the first time that all the strangers I had seen for years—the man with the seeing-eye dog, the spinster who read the classified pages every day, the fat girl who always got off with me at Grand Central—looked older than they once had." Perhaps this was a projection of her own fatigue. By then, what had once been extraordinary now seemed ordinary, what had once been ordinary now felt repetitive, and Didion saw that she had overstayed her time.

Didion left New York at the age of twenty-eight, saying she felt old. I arrived at that same age, still feeling very young. As a graduate student in creative writing, I lucked into a three-bedroom apartment share a half block from the Film Forum, four blocks from Washington Square Park, and a short walk in any direction to great cafés, bookstores, and fresh bread. With a teaching stipend of $11,000, I couldn't afford—nor did I crave—a whole lot more. My stabilized rent of $528 a month allowed me to enjoy that modest lifestyle without sinking too far into debt. Thus would I remain in an increasingly difficult roommate situation far longer than I should have. Only after Hurricane Sandy swept through, and my roommate bounced me from the apartment, was I forced to leave a stressful environment that I'd been too timid to abandon on my own.

What a blessing that was. My move to Brooklyn gave me a new lease on the city—as did the move I made eight and a half years later: from Brooklyn back to Manhattan. In my third chapter of living in New York, I finally felt reliably situated. I was a homeowner, which put me beyond the whims of greedy landlords, unmanageable roommates, and ever-inflating rents. My current apartment was on Third Avenue overlooking 18th Street. The area was too far north to be in the East Village; too far east to count as Union Square; too far south to be in Midtown; and just far enough from Gramercy to feel out of its orbit. And yet my new neighborhood was anything but a no-man's-land. Between Third Avenue and Union Square lay a number of pleasant side streets lined with attractive apartments, shapely front stoops, and colorful flower boxes. There was also Irving Place, a charming six-block street that ran parallel to Union Square and dead-ended at Gramercy Park. The charming stretch boasted a cheese shop, a garden-level café like a London tea parlor, an outrageously popular ice cream shop, and Pete's Tavern—one of the city's oldest drinking establishments and a regular hangout for the short-story writer O. Henry.

One block east of me, between 15th and 17th Street, lay a small park of unsuspecting beauty. It was flanked on three sides by stylish apartments, a classic red-brick school building of the Quaker Friends, and the elegant brownstone church of St. George's Episcopal. From almost anywhere inside the park, you could see the church's large roseate window and two square bell towers perched above the trees. Tiled walking paths spread through the park's many small gardens and converged on a center fountain that was ringed with flowers. Just off to the side, a tall bronze statue kept watch from the nearby trees. It was Peter Stuyvesant, the park's namesake and onetime director general of the New Netherlands. Donning his colonial garb, bearing himself proudly in spite of his peg leg, the man cupped his palm atop his walking stick like an arrogant homerun hitter in the on-deck circle.

To stroll these paths in summertime was to feel transported to an era of premodern gentility. And yet you couldn't help feeling a cross breeze of the Quaker egalitarian spirit. Unlike the private park in Gramercy, Stuyvesant Square happily admitted all-comers. That included an unlikely species I happened to spot one Saturday morning, the likes of which I'd never seen before. Entering from 15th Street with my usual cup of coffee, I noticed an unusual four-legged animal a little ways down the path. This dusky, barrel-shaped creature wore a purple harness over its shoulders and was being led by a woman in short denim overalls. From a distance, with its light-colored hooves, string bean tail, and broad snout, the animal resembled a mini-hippopotamus. Its snout swept over the paving stones like a metal detector, and I soon recognized what the other park goers were taking pictures of or lingering to get a better look at. The owner herself, riveted to her cell phone, seemed totally oblivious to the attention. She might've been pushing a baby stroller or walking a golden retriever, like so many others on that Saturday morning, instead of chaperoning a large pig by a purple leash under the watchful gaze of Peter Stuyvesant.

***

If burnout made for one kind of refugee, the dramatic pace of change made for another. From my earliest days on Houston Street, I watched as the downtown skyline gradually reshaped itself. Glass and steel buildings went up where they didn't belong. Outsized towers thumbed their noses at their shorter neighbors. New York University, the grad school I attended, played no small role in this upheaval. I saw longtime residents walking around in T-shirts that read: I Live in NYU Village Which Used To Be Greenwich Village. At the border of the West Village, the Hudson waterfront also came under threat. Modern condos sprung up like invasive species, only to be mirrored by those taking root on New Jersey's opposite shoreline, as if in some combined project to resemble Hong Kong. Community members didn't fail to speak out. I attended one public hearing where an architect tried to defend a hideous building that was totally out of sync with the neighborhood. In front of a packed, hostile audience, he argued for what he called an "adjusted context," floating that term with a straight face like he was trying to pull off a Jedi mind trick.

Twenty years later, the annals of lost places were too long to record. There were famous institutions like Tower Records and Le Figaro Café, plus small neighborhood joints like Pizza Box or the fruit and vegetable market on Bleecker Street. One day, an independent movie theater might fall. The next day, a cherished bakery or bookstore would hang a CLOSED sign in its window. Every time a shop went under, you felt a small piece of yourself disappear as well. Sometimes, in a matter of only a few months, a familiar street would suddenly look unfamiliar. Then another. The spread of chain pharmacies and bank branches stripped certain blocks of their character and created a sad, monochromatic feel, like the bleaching of a coral reef.

The longer I spent in New York, the more I felt the grip of its past. I started to think and sound like my father, remarking on which store used to be over here, which building used to stand over there. On East 11th near Veniero's Bakery, I still caught myself hunting for remnants of the old Cinema Classics, be it a stray movie poster or some peeling show bill not yet scraped away by time. A similar feeling accompanied me at Bleecker and West 11th, the former home of Biography Bookshop, which I used to pop into on my night-time strolls through the West Village. The bookstore was the very definition of what Hemingway called a "clean, well-lighted place." On East 6th Street, between First and Second Avenue, you'd never guess that the entire south side of the block was once dominated by low-priced Indian restaurants. Back then, the running joke was that every restaurant secretly shared the same rear kitchen, so it didn't matter which place you went to for rogan josh, saag paneer, or the popular chicken tikka masala.

And yet that wasn't the only trend. The city that taketh away was also a city that giveth. Many long years after the Grey Dog gave up its canine constituency, I found those beloved pets cavorting at an East Village café called Boris & Horton. The owners managed this feat by dividing the service area from the dining area by a short hallway with a door at each end. Other exciting places also sprang up. On East 3rd Street I discovered a bookstore-café called Book Club, which turned into a wine bar after dark and stayed open until midnight. Then there was Plantshed, a coffee shop that doubled as a plant store—or a plant store that doubled as a coffee shop. Such places moved into the neighborhood like distant relatives, bringing in an immediate sense of kinship and helping reverse the effects of other unfortunate closures.

Whenever a new lead turned up, I still traded scouting reports with my friend and fellow cyclist from the old days on Houston Street. Way back when, neither of us ever predicted that biking would one day evolve from a fringe activity to become mainstream. Which didn't mean that everyone gave cyclists their proper respect. Many New Yorkers still regarded us like pigeons: creatures you shared space with only grudgingly, and only because you'd never get rid of them all. I'd seen that attitude in the city's own bus drivers. Imagine riding your bike down Fifth Avenue when a studio apartment on wheels lumbers past you, only to slip into your lane and risk turning you into roadkill. Imagine the added insult when its rear end swings into view, and you notice—stamped between the tail lights—the perfectly obnoxious question: How Am I Driving?

***

The subject of leaving felt like part of the natural cycle of living here. Even native New Yorkers weren't immune. Fetching back to two of Woody Allen's best movies, *Annie Hall* and *Manhattan*, the characters are beset by the city's professional, economic, and social pressures. Some hold fast and cling to their beloved city. Others throw in the towel and move on. Those movies came out in the late 1970s, when crime was way up in New York, the city was teetering on bankruptcy, and films like *Taxi Driver* exposed the grim decline. The variables might change, but it seemed like every several years, some profound event would touch the city as a whole, some catastrophe would generate an outsized ripple effect, and the issue of leaving would percolate all over again. During those times, many more people step back to reconsider what the term quality of life truly means to them, and just how much they're willing to give up for it.

The first event on my watch was 9/11. After two hijacked planes rammed into the Twin Towers and reduced the city's tallest buildings to rubble, a lingering foul air, plus a lingering fear of terrorism, drove many people out of lower Manhattan. Some fled the city altogether. The issue of leaving came back during the Great Recession, when the economy cratered, unemployment doubled, and people decried runaway speculation on Wall Street. It resurfaced again after Hurricane Sandy, when the superstorm wreaked havoc on the city and drove home fears about rising sea levels. Those worries seemed to have receded since then, but for me they returned a couple years ago, while I was watching Neil deGrasse Tyson on an episode of *Real Time With Bill Maher*. The famous astrophysicist declared—with the confidence of a man who knew Earth's exact orbital distance around the Sun—that if the polar ice sheets were to melt, the ocean waters would reach as high as the elbow on the Statue of Liberty. He didn't say which elbow, but we all got the point.

Then came COVID. The pandemic grabbed an early foothold in New York, killing thousands and sickening thousands more. The coronavirus parked freezer trucks in front of hospitals as holding tanks for the dead. It spread homeless encampments to nearly every zip code. The newspapers trafficked in daily death counts and infection rates, while they ran such stories as "Are Cities a Safe Place to Live During a Pandemic?" and "New Yorkers Are Fleeing to the Suburbs: 'The Demand Is Insane.'" With a highly transmissible virus on the loose, people wondered if living shoulder-to-shoulder in a city of millions was really worth the benefits. A great number of them decided it wasn't.

And yet a mass exodus never ensued. As with 9/11, people hunkered down and felt a tremendous loyalty to where they lived. Such a rallying effect was described by numerous interviews in a *Gothamist* story titled, "On Why They Love NYC, Now More Than Ever." As people rode the subway less and stayed closer to home, they felt even more connected to their neighborhoods. In a *New York Times* op-ed ("So You Think NY Is Dead"), comedian Jerry Seinfeld took on the city's detractors while standing up for the very *idea* of New York. He argued that its "Energy, attitude and personality" were not traits you could obtain remotely, or in what he sarcastically called the "creative spirit" that was Florida. Those qualities, he reminded his readers, were "the whole reason many of us moved to New York in the first place."

The topic of leaving came up every so often among friends. Was the city that had given us so much inspiration and so many tentacles of opportunity still the best place to meet our artistic goals? A few years ago, when I was at a small dinner party in the East Village, the question reared its head again at a profound moment in my own journey.

I was still living in Brooklyn at the time. From Borough Hall I took the 4 train to Union Square, where I hopped a Citi Bike and rode down to East 10th Street—my favorite pipeline into the East Village. This was in the summertime, when East 10th became a forested thruway, offering a change in scenery from block to block. After Third Avenue, you passed a run of fancy townhouses reminiscent of the Henry James era; then the handsomely austere St. Mark's Church, with its broad white portico and massive steeple. This was followed by a stretch of old tenement buildings with roofline cornices, pediment windows, and carved keystones. Just before you reached Avenue A, a stunning red-brick building suddenly loomed on your right. It was the Saint Nicholas of Myra Orthodox Church. The building looked like a cross between a monastery and a psychiatric hospital, with an imposing sanctuary of stained glass, imperial lancet windows, and a rooftop bell tower that resembled a sniper's perch.

Thereafter, Tompkins Square Park opened broadly along 10th Street and Avenue A. From the spread of trees came the rumble of skateboards running up and down ramps, the clap of hockey sticks against the pavement. In the summertime, as the afternoons drained slowly toward sunset and the park life melded with the gathering nightlife, you felt like you'd entered the beating heart of the East Village. Car horns wailed impatiently along Avenue A, loud music spilled from the bars and restaurants. People trickled in and out of the park's many entrances like an oversized ant colony, which seemed to create and absorb the very commotion that surrounded it.

Only a few short blocks away, my friends' apartment felt shielded from these many vibrations. The building's shared courtyard was mostly concealed from the street, and it was in this side garden that our evening began. We sat under a thin tree at a large patio table, where the hosts served snacks and offered a choice of Pimm's, rosé, or white wine. Dinner was a spicy rice-and-beans dish, accompanied by a salad of fresh ingredients from the farm cooperative they belonged to. A few citronella candles gave protection from the mosquitoes, but there was no defense against the sudden and unexpected downpour. Everyone scurried for cover under the wooden staircase flanking the building, hoping for a passing shower, but after a few minutes we were forced to gather up everything in a mad scramble and bring the party indoors.

Once inside, the talk shifted as suddenly as the weather. The breeziness of outdoor conversation gave way to a range of deeper subjects: topics we would spend the rest of the night unpacking. Everyone had their own story about family. There were difficult or neglectful siblings, in-laws who'd grown cross with one family member or fallen out with another. None of our parents had stopped aging, but that didn't make them more receptive to the extra care they now required. The burdens of back home, no matter what form they took, felt similarly intractable. Everyone had a friend or relative they couldn't talk politics with anymore. Everyone had lost at least one childhood acquaintance to a movement that seemed deeply hostile to facts and science, and that denied the existence of a pandemic that was decimating its own members.

Amid these turbulent seas, New York still felt like a safe harbor. The members of our group that evening included fiction writers, screenwriters, fashion writers, current or former teachers, and proofreaders. Each of us wore at least a couple of different hats, and we all pulled our income from at least a couple of different sources. The end of summer wasn't that far off, and the teachers discussed our upcoming courses before we broadened the topic to the more general state of education. Even non-teachers could see the trend. The classroom had become a much shakier place in recent years, with students triggered far more frequently and their complaints far more supercharged than ever. For many students, freedom of expression had become the ruling principle, which meant that any talk of basic skills or discipline would land as flat as a straight edge on a desktop.

From the state of our students' work, we turned to the fate of our own. We talked about projects that were currently in progress and projects that were still bumping around in our heads. We bounced ideas off one another—partly to hear everyone else's feedback, partly to affirm that we hadn't yet run out of ideas. Everyone agreed it was a constant struggle to bring your work to a larger audience. Whether you were trying to publish a book or turn a screenplay into a movie, it took endless hustle and dogged persistence to get across the finish line. At some point, in the ebb and flow of this discussion, we drifted downstream into deeper water. Someone raised the question of what else we might be doing with our lives—if we weren't doing X or Y—and where else we might be doing it.

It felt like a small projectile had landed in the room. The question forced everyone to ask themselves: Was New York really necessary to the life we'd chosen, or did staying in New

York give us the excuse to continue with that life? I thought back on my arrival twenty years ago, and how so much—and so little—seemed to have changed since then. I was no longer that young graduate student getting his feet wet, and yet every time I went to the keyboard, I still felt very much like that same person. I was a writer who squirreled about between commas, who would scavenge for words that seemed buried under leaves or hidden behind rocks. Too often I would miss the forest for the twigs. Too frequently, I worried my writing didn't meet the tastes of a reading public. Hadn't I been warned about this from the beginning? To the aspiring writers in his craft of fiction class, E.L. Doctorow had testified about how little trust people had in the written word. This was way back in the early 2000s: a time when Facebook, iPhones, and Instagram were still a thing of the future. Even then, Doctorow had told us that we were living in an age when much of what people read, they were already reading online—and much of what they were reading was already bolstered by photos, links, or other visuals. In the years to come, the plight of the written word would only get worse.

And yet that wasn't the full story either. Doctorow had cautioned us about the perils of our trade, but he'd layered his words with encouragement as well. He'd told us to write without intention. Write, he said, in order to discover the very thing we were trying to write about. Those words had made a lasting impression on me. Not only did they define each project along the way, but they seemed to define the larger trajectory I'd taken. Behind me lay a long trail of happy accidents and dead ends, a pathway of surprising twists and misleading turns. I saw work that I could hang my hat on with some pride, and plenty more that was embarrassing or stubbornly unfixable. Ahead of me, the path looked as obscure and ill-defined as ever. That was certainly the case with the latest project I'd been working on, but so was my burning desire to see where it would take me.

The project was a blend of something new and something old. It was a mix of stories from my early years in the city with stories that were still evolving in the present tense. A bookshelf's worth of journals had recorded these events. The pages were a chronicle of intriguing characters I'd met, movies I'd seen, fabulous episodes I'd witnessed or been part of. They told of my encounters with celebrities, politicians, and other writers; of dustups with cabbies and unrepentant truck drivers. They described the amusing rituals and quirky run-ins of café goers; the inspiring but sometimes embattled life of the classroom; and the daily struggle to be creative in an ever-changing, ever-gentrifying city.

It was my story, but it was also the story of something much larger. If journalism was said to be the first draft of history, then I considered my journals the first draft of history and memoir. Wasn't there a sense of destiny in those pages? They recorded events that had transformed both the city and the broader direction of our country. I had witnessed tragic episodes like 9/11 and the coronavirus, a great recession and a great hurricane. I had seen Arthur Miller in the twilight of his career, when the playwright shared a tale of childhood bigotry and warned of a centuries-old intolerance that would continue beyond his lifespan. Years later, after a bitter presidential election, that hatred would hit close to home in a rash of swastikas on my local playground. It would show its ugly face at a neo-Nazi rally in Charlottesville, Virginia; in a mass shooting at a Pittsburgh synagogue; and in the stabbing of a rabbi in Monsey, New York.

Back and forth, the pendulum had swung over the years. In Manhattan, I had marched against the Iraq War and in support of climate action. In Brooklyn, I had seen a small army of policemen protecting Jews at a *No Hate. No Fear.* rally. At the very same plaza, after the murder of George Floyd in Minneapolis, I had taken a knee against racial injustice and police brutality. Over the course of a single evening, I had felt the pendulum swing ever so slightly in real time. An afternoon run and a stroke of luck had brought me to Washington Square Park, where I joined a crowd of twenty thousand in listening to a young senator from my home state of Illinois. This gifted speaker would light a fire under his audience that night, spread that same electricity throughout the country, and become the first African American to occupy the White House.

This was my story, but it was also the story of my father. Almost everywhere I turned, I discovered overlaps with his own time here. Some were more predictable, like my trips to Katz's Deli or the Film Forum, where I'd watch a movie like *Purple Noon* or *The Naked City*, some picture my dad had seen a half century earlier and still recalled in which theater. Other times, that synergy would strike by accident. It happened once while I was visiting an orthopedist on the Upper East Side, and the name of a random high-rise jumped out at me from across the street. Here was the building we'd lived in when my father was just starting his career, the apartment whose large blue nursery room became my first childhood memory. Then there was the small Catholic mission on East 3rd Street, which I'd ducked my head inside to inquire about volunteering. Only a couple weeks later, while texting with my father from a nearby café, I learned that those two adjoining townhouses with the peeling red paint were the very same address as my father's old music school: the place he'd gone to for his first piano lessons as a young boy.

How to explain all this to my friends that evening? I didn't know where to begin, as I wasn't even sure what shape the book would take, or how the storylines would pull together. The party stretched on well past midnight. The rains came softly to an end, and it turned into one of those fairy-tale evenings when the hours melted away, you felt transported by your company, and you probably drank a few more glasses than you should have. After our goodbyes were said, I was carried out the door on a wave of euphoria. It seemed unthinkable to take the subway, so instead I jumped a Citi Bike from a nearby docking station. The streets glistened softly from leftover rain. I rode down Avenue B past Houston Street, down through the Lower East Side and past the old street names that were so familiar to my father and grandfather. In Chinatown, I pivoted through the empty lanes and past the exotic storefronts until I turned onto Lafayette Street, where I pedaled past the ghostly-white courthouses and sprawling stone palace that was City Hall. Just beyond these buildings, merging left onto the slim bike path, I turned my handlebars and pointed them toward the Brooklyn Bridge.

The path changed to wooden planks as it ascended. Around me grew a magnificent cabled webbing, carving up the scenery that lined both sides of the East River. A few pedestrians had stopped along the railing. Some took selfies or shot videos, others held hands or passed a joint back and forth. The path leveled off at some point, and between the stone towers I found a quiet spot to dismount. A glittering, breathtaking view spread out in all directions. My head turned on a swivel as I took in the neighboring skylines of Brooklyn and Manhattan, the distant speckled lights out on the harbor. It was in this moment, as had happened countless times before, that I was visited again by thoughts of my father. A sudden shiver ran through me. I felt separate from all the other travelers on that famous bridge: separate from my fellow sightseers and all the other late-night commuters. The place I occupied was entirely my own. No one else could've occupied it. High above the East River, suspended between boroughs, I stood between a world of tomorrow and a vision from my father's past. I was a grown-up son inhabiting a city of the future: a New York City that my father, as an excitable young boy some eighty years ago, could only dream about.

END

Acknowledgments

I'M GRATEFUL TO JIM MCCARTHY, agent extraordinaire, for his tremendous stewardship and endless encouragement throughout this whole process. He is a saint! I'm deeply thankful to the whole team at Post Hill—Deborah Englander, Caitlin Burdette, HB Steadman, Cody Corcoran, and everyone else—for their hard work in making this book the best version of itself.

I can't begin to express my appreciation for all the kindness and support of friends and former mentors: Bret Anthony Johnston, Jacob Appel, John Melnick and the entire Melnick family, Natalie Friedman, Randon Noble, Chris Momenee, Jacqueline Mallon, Pascal Agostini, Susan and Sheldon Gottlieb, Dan Gottlieb, Heidi Berry, Matt Solomon, Jason Robertshaw, Martin Schroeder, Scott Wiper, Jason and Stacie Primer, Joe Romano, Patricia Lymes, Caroline Beeland, Bart Mullin, Brian Morton, Albert Mobilio, Pat Hoy, Denice Martone, and Darlene Forrest.

Some chapters of this book appeared previously in slightly different versions or under different names. In *The American Scholar*: "September 11th, 2001," "Confessions of a Cyclist," "E.L. Doctorow and the Writer in the Family." In *Tablet Magazine*: "Second Avenue Elevated." My thanks to the very wise and extremely dedicated editors at these journals: Sudip Bose, Jayne Ross, and Matthew Fishbane.

With love and eternal gratitude for my parents, Philip and Carole.

Permissions

From A Walker In The City by Alfred Kazin. Copyright (c) 1951, 1946 by Alfred Kazin, Copyright renewed (c) 1979, 1974 by Alfred Kazin. Used by permission of HarperCollins Publishers.

From "Here is New York" by E.B. White. Copyright (c) White Literary LLC, 1949, 1976. Reprinted by permission of White Literary LLC.

From On Bicycles: A 200-Year History of Cycling in New York by Evan Friss. Copyright (c) 2019 Columbia University. Reprinted with permissions of Columbia University.

From Lives of the Poets by E.L. Doctorow. Copyright (c) 1984. Reprinted with permissions from Penguin Random House LLC.

Excerpts from "On Keeping a Notebook" and "Goodbye to All That" from SLOUCHING TOWARDS BETHLEHEM by Joan Didion. Copyright © 1966, 1968, renewed 1996 by Joan Didion. Reprinted by permission of Farrar, Straus and Giroux. All Rights Reserved.

About the Author

Jonathan Liebson grew up in suburban Chicago and earned a BA from Wesleyan University, an MA from the University of Kent (UK), and an MFA in fiction from New York University, where he was a fellow in expository writing. He currently lives in New York and teaches courses on writing, literature, and culture at Eugene Lang College of Liberal Arts at The New School. He's taught previously at NYU, Gotham Writers Workshop, College of Charleston, and Miami of Ohio.

Liebson's writing and reviews have appeared in *The Atlantic*, *The Washington Post*, *The American Scholar*, *Tablet Magazine*, *Time Out NY*, and *Naming the World: And Other Exercises for the Creative Writer* (Random House), and has been selected for the InterAct Theatre Company's *Writing Aloud* series, in Philadelphia.

www.ingramcontent.com/pod-product-compliance
Ingram Content Group UK Ltd.
Pitfield, Milton Keynes, MK11 3LW, UK
UKHW021651190726
13853UKWH00001B/200